SARDAR VALLABHBHAI PATEL

The Maker of United India

SARDAR VALLABHBHAI PATEL

The Maker of United India

Editor
Dr. Ravindra Kumar

GYAN

GYAN PUBLISHING HOUSE
NEW DELHI - 110002

Sardar Vallabhbhai Patel: The Maker of United India

ISBN: 978-81-212-0874-1

Price: ₹ 700

Reprinted 2015 in India by
Gyan Publishing House
23, Main Ansari Road, Daryaganj,
New Delhi - 110002
Phones : 23282060, 23261060
Fax : (011) 23285914
E-mail: books@gyanbooks.com
Website: gyanbooks.com

Printed at: G. Print Process, Delhi

Contents

ABBREVIATIONS

A. I. C.C.	: All India Congress Committee
C. W. C.	: Congress Working Committee
G. P. C. C.	: Gujarat *Prantik* [Provincial] Congress Committee
I. A. S.	: Indian Administrative Service
I. C. S.	: Indian Civil Service
I. F. S.	: Indian Foreign Service
I. P. S.	: Indian Police Service
U. P.	: Uttar Pradesh

Our Duty

"In every State, people demand Responsible Government. The rulers are aware of it and they know that they have to march with the times. At the same time, we should also be clear about our duty. It is our right to take over Government from them, but if we cannot improve upon it and provide better administration, what is the gain."

—Sardar Vallabhbhai Patel

For a Strong, Prosperous and Happy India

"I make earnest appeal to people to wipe out from their minds and memories of the past-treating it as a terrible nightmare and look forward with single minded purpose to make India strong, prosperous and happy. This can only be done by hard work."

—Sardar Vallabhbhai Patel

Foreword

Sardar Vallabhbhai Patel was one of the key players in the creation of newly independent India. Sadly, I never met him in person because, like Mahatma Gandhi, he had died before my first visit to India in 1956. Nevertheless, I am aware of his great reputation, particularly of his work to bring together the far-flung parts of India and forge a united nation. In Tibet, the great Fifth Dalai Lama is similarly remembered with affection and respect for the same reason.

Known for his determination and fortitude, Sardar Patel was also astute and farsighted. He was greatly concerned about the future of Tibet and tried to warn Prime Minister Nehru about the threat of the Chinese Communist invasion of Tibet.

Sardar Patel was a man of courage and vision, determined to take up the challenge and provide guidance. His sense of self-sacrifice was typical of the freedom fighters of his generation. Who could fail to be impressed by someone who made his principles clear with these words?

"I cannot speak anything but the truth. I cannot turn back on my duty, just to please someone."

We need leaders of such calibre and dedication today. I hope that the publication of this book of Dr. Ravindra Kumar about the great man will inspire young people especially to follow in his footsteps.

-Tensin Gyatso
The 14th Dalai Lama

List of Contributors

1. Mr. Manohar Joshi is the Former Speaker of Lok Sabha [Lower House of the Indian Parliament].
2. Dr. Yogendra Narayan, a Senior I.A.S. is currently the General Secretary of Rajya Sabha [Upper House of the Indian Parliament].
3. Mr. Shankar Sinh Vaghela is a Union Minister of India. He is also the Former Chief-Minister of Gujarat State.
4. Dr. Manoj Ratilal Soni is the Director of Sardar Vallabhbhai Patel Centre, Sardar Patel University, Vallabh Vidyanagar [Gujarat].
5. Mr. B.J. Patel is a veteran freedom fighter, Gandhian and a senior statesman from Gujarat. He has been the Chief Minister of Gujarat between 1975 and 1979.
6. Dr. Raj Kumar Kothari teaches Political Science at the Jogesh Chandra Chaudhuri College, Kolkata.
7. Mr. J.N. Chaturvedi is a Senior I.P.S. Officer from U.P. [India].
8. Dr. Amit Dholakia is a Senior Lecturer in Political Science, Faculty of Arts, The M.S. University of Baroda, Vadodara [India].
9. Dr. S.V.D. Paul is the Head of the D.I.E.T., Tamil Nadu [India].
10. Professor M. Mehta is a noted Economist from Ahmedabad [Gujarat].

11. Dr. Mehboob Desai is a Reader Department of History, and Director of Gandhian Studies Centre, Bhavnagar University, Bhavnagar, [Gujarat].
12. Dr. Rizwan Kadri is a Lecturer in History at Shri Swaminarayan Arts College, Ahmedabad.
13. Professor Johannes D. Schmidt is the Director, Institute of International Studies, Aalborg University, Denmark.
14. Professor Shirin Mehta, a noted Scholar and Professor from Gujarat University, Ahmedabad [India].
15. Mr. B. Satyanarayan Reddy is a veteran freedom fighter and socialist leader. Between 1990 and 1995 he was the Governor of Uttar Pradesh and Orissa.
16. Dr. Paitoon Patyaiying is the Former Head of Department of Philosophy and Religion, Faculty of Humanities and Social Sciences, Prince of Songkla University, Southern Thailand. Also he is an eminent Indologist and the author of a number of books.
17. Mr. P.P. Rao is a senior advocate of Supreme Court of India
18. Mr. Sachin Bathla is a Cultural Anthropologist and author. He is also the Assistant Editor of 'Global Peace' - an International Journal of Philosophy, Peace, Education, Culture and Civilization.
19. Dr. Anjula Rajvanshi is an Assistant Professor at the Department of Sociology, RG (PG) College, CCS University, Meerut, [India].
20. Mr. Jayant Oza is the Director and Secretary of Sardar Patel Trust, Sardar Vallabhbhai Patel and Veer Vithalbhai Patel Memorial, Karamsad, Gujarat, India
21. Mr. Bhupesh Bhatt is an Assistant Professor at the BIMT, [India].

22. Professor Dr. Karin Preisendanz is the Director of the I.I., University of Vienna, Austria.
23. Dr. Ravindra Kumar is the former Vice-Chancellor of CCS University, Meerut [India]. Also he is the Editor-in-Chief of 'Global-Peace'-an international journal of philosophy, peace, education, culture and civilization.
24. The late N.V. alias Kakasaheb Gadgil- a right-hand of Sardar Patel was a top ranking freedom fighter and the Congress leader from Maharashtra who became a Minister in the First Cabinet of independent India [1947], headed by Pt. Nehru. He was appointed the Governor of undivided Punjab in 1958.

INTRODUCTION

Sardar Vallabhbhai Patel – the maker of united India died 54 years ago. But still he is alive in social and political fields of India. It is but natural. It is the outcome of achievements which Sardar Patel acquired for the nation and the society. On one hand, he is considered to be a practical person like Mahatma Gandhi, while on the other; he has a status of a leading figure with real and effective thinking among his contemporaries. His practical approach to problems always had their rewards and it was truly so when, as a master strategist, he suggested some very prompt and effective measures at the meeting of representatives of Punjab States on September 26, 1947 in nipping retaliatory evil in the bud gathering momentum in these particularly affected parts of the country. To quote one from his important suggestions:

"Province of East Punjab and the Central Government should all lend their hands without any motive of profit or selfish gain, but actuated entirely by a desire to assist in a humanitarian cause."

Sardar Patel merged 554 scattered and odd princely states with the Indian Union through a proper and efficient way in a short span of time. It was not an easy task. It was indeed a great job. In the entire history of India the task of such kind of solidarity had never been done before. That is why Dr. Rajendra Prasad had said:

"That there is an India, to think and talk about, is very largely due to Sardar Patel's statesmanship and firm administration".

After independence, besides creating political unity of India, Sardar Patel played vital role in the Constituent Assembly; he handled the serious problems pertaining to accession, law and order, exchange of population, and made arrangements for rehabilitation of *crores* of refugees. To make the bureaucracy fully responsible Vallabhbhai raised two services - Indian Administrative and Indian Police Service. All these works of Sardar Patel were so great and unique that no person can accomplish them in his one lifetime. However, Vallabhbhai accomplished them. It is also true that a person like him is born once in thousands of years.

Perhaps the present generation would like to know how Sardar Patel was able to carry out such big tasks. I would like to mention that he could do so because he was capable of taking quick and appropriate decision. He always contemplated seriously before taking any decision but after reaching a decision he implemented it. He had a unique art to do so.

It was not that Sardar Patel completed any task on his own. Many of his colleagues, co-workers and subordinates stood with him in performing the job. He always maintained faith among his colleagues and co-workers; encouraged them on every step. It was a good basis of success. In this regard, paying tribute to Sardar Vallabhbhai Patel, Pandit Jawaharlal Nehru had said in the Parliament on 15 December 1950:

"Vallabhbhai Patel will always be remembered as the commander of our forces in the struggle for freedom. He was such a person who always gave just and right advice whether it was a time of crisis or a moment of victory. He was such a friend, comrade and colleague on whom we could undoubtedly rely

as a mountain of strength that filled our hearts with energy in the time of trouble."

Which work is to be done and which not, Sardar used to take decision for it keeping national interest in his mind. He laid great emphasis that the interest of the nation should be seen with far sightedness. That is why his colleagues and co-workers were in union with him. They, being united, were ready to achieve their goals. For this reason a difficult task also became easy.

Today we need to learn too many things from the life and work of Sardar Vallabhbhai Patel - a man of multi dimensional personality. It is necessary to follow his style of working and his way of thinking if we are sincere to the unity and solidarity of our country. From this point of view this work would be of great importance.

I am grateful to Mr. Manohar Joshi, Dr. Yogendra Narayan, Professor Dr. Mehboob Desai, Mr. B. J. Patel, Mr. Shankar Sinh Vaghela, Professor Dr. Makrand Mehta, Dr. Raj Kumar Kothari, Professor Dr. Shirin Mehta, Mr. B. Satyanarayan Reddy, Dr. Manoj Ratilal Soni, Professor Dr. Johannes Dragsbaek Schmidt, Dr. Rizwan Kadri, Dr. Anil Dholakia, Dr. S. V. De Paul, Mr. J. N. Chaturvedi, Mr. P. P. Rao, Mr. Jayant Oza, Dr. Bhupesh Bhatt, Dr. Anjula Rajvanshi, Dr. Paitoon Patyaiying, Mr. Sachin Bathla and Professor Dr. Karin Preisendanz for contributing their most valuable articles, to His Holiness the 14th Dalai Lama Tensin Gyatso for writing a Foreword for this work and to the officials of Sardar Vallabhbhai Patel and Veer Vithalbhai Patel Memorial [Sardar Patel Trust], Karamsad, especially its Director, Mr. Jayant Oza; and Former Secretary, Mr. Hasmukh M. Patel for their inspiration and providing assistance during preparation of this manuscript.

Besides, I am, especially, thankful to Miss Megha Khurana and Mr. Ramesh Prajapati who have extended their help to me in reading the manuscript.

In the end, I would like to mention about two articles that have been included in the end of this volume. Based on Kakasaheb Gadgil's reminiscences of Sardar Vallabhbhai Patel, these articles have been found in his papers during preparation of the manuscript of the Volume-V [1949-50] of his Selected Works. In one of these articles titled, 'Vallabhbhai', Kakasaheb Gadgil has mentioned about Sardar Patel's great work for the nation and has concluded:

"Sardar Saheb has offered the lotus of his life at the feet of Bharat Mata."

Ravindra Kumar

1

SARDAR PATEL: THE IRON MAN OF INDIA

-Manohar Joshi

Sardar Patel belongs to the galaxy of stalwarts whose forceful personality and shining leadership has been a source of inspiration for our countrymen. He gave to our freedom struggle a practical and organizational leadership. He was actively involved in the protest against the Rowlett Act in 1919 and in the Non-Cooperation Movement in 1920. His ardent patriotism, deep devotion to the people of India, and sacrifices in the cause of the nation are written in the golden letters on the pages of our history.

With his deep understanding of men and matters, Sardar Patel, played a remarkable role in ensuring the merger of Princely States into the Union of India. His greatness lay in the skill and smoothness with which he completed the task of integration. It was this achievement, which earned him the title of the Iron Man of India. *Acharya* Vinoba Bhave has rightly pointed out in this regard:

"The Sardar united the country by bringing into its fold a large number of Princely States. In history,

this will go down as an unparalleled piece of Sardar's service to the Motherland."

A man of strong determination will and clear vision, Sardar Patel left an indelible impression of his personality on our country and its people. His life and lofty ideas will continue to inspire and guide us, and the generations to come to build a vibrant, strong and prosperous India and to reserve and protest the hard-earned freedom and the integrity of the country.

It was Sardar Vallabhbhai Patel who rightly said:

"Obedience to law should be the fundamental duty of a citizen."[1]

From this also we can easily judge his burning desire and commitment for a strong India.

Needless to say, it is only by strengthening the fabric of our national unity that we can repay our immeasurable debt of Sardar Patel.

Reference

1. Quoted from Sardar Patel's speech dated 25.02.1950 in Parliament on the Preventive Detention Bill. The Bill had significance in the context of the subversive activities of the diehard people. By virtue of the new liberal and democratic Constitution of the country, such subversive elements in the absence of a measure of this kind could go scot-free. That had not only affected the law and order situation and brought it into disrepute but it had also cast its malicious effect on the mind of masses in the country. By introduction of this Bill, Sardar Vallabhbhai Patel, while maintaining the spirit of the Constitution, sought to arrest this evil growth by legislative action. If one cares to study the sporadic activities of those people and the anti-social elements both from the point of defence and internal security to life, one would definitely realize as to why Sardar Vallabhbhai Patel introduced this Bill as an expedient measure. One can read his mind when he said in his speech by introducing the Bill: "When we think of civil liberties of the extremely small number of persons concerned, the House also think of the liberties of the millions of people threatened by the activities of individuals whose civil liberties we have curtailed. See appendix-B for details of the speech.

2

A Tribute to the Memory and Vision of Sardar Patel

Yogendra Narayan

Rarely in the history of a nation, does a personality of the stature and standing of Sardar Vallabhbhai Patel emerge, to fashion its destiny as an outstanding soldier in its struggle for independence and subsequently as a remarkable leader and architect of its integration and unification. British rulers, apart from preparing a diabolical plan for dividing India into Hindustan and Pakistan had also formulated a sinister strategy to create what was called a Princes-stan, primarily consisting of the erstwhile princely states of India. The problems of bringing the princely states to the mainstream of nationalist movement for independence and integrating them to the Indian union had threatened our national unity. Many of our top leaders then found the issue formidable and daunting. Mahatma Gandhi with rare clairvoyance had written to Sardar Patel in 1939:

"The problem of the states is so difficult that you alone can solve it."

Sardar Patel's vision, statesmanship, astute statecraft and practical action foiled the British plan of breaking

India into pieces and forever put an end to the obnoxious doctrine of paramountcy which established the unassailed supremacy of British interests over the interests of Indians. India was in her meridian splendour when the princely states were integrated to the Indian union and the paramountcy of people's interests was restored and we authentically affirmed our unity and integrity for the first time in our long history.

Our first President Dr. Rajendra Prasad acknowledging Sardar Patel's contribution in integrating India wrote in 1952:

"That there is an India, to think and talk about, is very largely due to Sardar Patel's statesmanship and firm administration."

In fact it was Sardar Patel who imparted leadership and direction to the administrative structure of independent India and infused with it the new purpose of national reconstruction and development. Acclaiming the faithful, devoted and splendid service of administrators he went to the extent of saying that without them India would have been overwhelmed by chaos, anarchy and disorder. To the Members of the Constituent Assembly who felt agitated and restless about the functioning of civil service and even questioned its loyalty, Sardar Patel said:

"Do not quarrel with the instruments with which you want to work. It is a bad workman who quarrels with the instrument. Nobody wants to put in work when he is criticized and ridiculed in public."

Sardar Patel, in spite of his exalted status as the Iron Man of India, was full of compassion and feeling for the common people of our country and exerted his energy for improving their living conditions. Even while fighting for freedom he underlined the importance of bringing about changes in society, which he thought required, concentrated attention and action. He had said:

"Social change is more valuable and difficult than fighting the government."

Sardar Patel had many great qualities of leadership. His mind could grasp complicated situations almost instantaneously. In the words of Dr. Rajendra Prasad:

"He could see things straight and after he had once considered and made up his mind on any matter, it was most difficult, if not impossible, to dislodge him. This does not mean that whenever one differed from him, one had to yield. If he had a different view on any particular point and he was pressed hard by his colleagues to take action in a contrary direction, he would not give up his own opinion but carry out the wishes of his colleagues. It was for this reason that he was known as the strong man of the Congress."

It was also a fact that once he undertook a job, he would see to it that it was done. Where differences were so acute that he could not himself do the things, he would simply keep quite and let others carry on.

He was a guide and philosopher of the Indian National Congress. He appealed to its members to close up their minds and apply themselves to complex problems of the country and with practical vision, discipline and an increasing sense of responsibility. In his message to the Bombay Session of the A. I. C. C. Session in 1948 he said:

"As an organization, therefore, we must be even more closely-knit and must now come nearer and nearer. Discipline and increasing sense of responsibility in what we say and what we do, a more practical approach to the problems and a greater regard for national as against parochial consideration would seem to be the need of the hour."

He also said:

"We have fought one of the greatest battles of freedom which had ever adorned the pages of history.

We fought it under the matchless inspiration and guidance of our departed leader. Let us keep alive the unity...and the indomitable spirit of that struggle. Let us keep burning the torch that great soul handed to us."

One of the lesser-known aspects of his life was that he advocated the cause of women and elicited their support and opinion before launching major movements against British rule. Shri Rajmohan Gandhi in his well-researched book "Patel" has brought to public knowledge that Vallabhbhai Patel remained a moving force behind the representation of Dr. B. R. Ambedkar in the Constituent Assembly. One of the distinguished aspects of Sardar Patel's life was his value-based approach to politics. Three years after our independence he was agonized by the distortions and disintegrations of our principles and standards of behaviour, which governed political and social spheres. On 15th August 1950 in a message to our people he rang the alarm bell by saying:

"Our public life seems to be degenerating into a fen of stagnant waters; our conscience is troubled with doubts and despair about the possibilities of improvement."

We can ignore such poignant words of Sardar Patel at our own peril. Recapturing the spirit of service and sacrifice of Sardar Patel and translating that to action would be a fitting tribute to his memory and vision.

3

SARDAR PATEL

Shankar Sinh Vaghela

Leadership in India today demands that human values should be honoured and the welfare of the downtrodden should be strengthened at the grassroots level. It demands an ethos that should have high ethical standards and combine justice and economic prosperity. What was the genius of Sardar Vallabhbhai Patel and his special contribution to the Congress movement? The well-known scholar M. H. Lyon in his book entitled, *"SARDAR PATEL AND INDIAN INDEPENDENCE"* puts it in proper perspective in the following words:

"The singular achievement of the Congress had laid in modernizing and mobilizing culture; in communicating at the grassroots and gathering support, on the widest possible national basis. It was when the original genius of this indigenous solution proved impossible to sustain that formal constitution powers became an inadequate substitute for consensus."

"Sardar Patel may be hailed as the strong man who erected the steel frame of state and so

constructed the permanent house of India. However, he was not satisfied to be an architect of the building. His paramount concern was to cultivate the nation, as an extended family, for living purpose."

The task that devolves on all of us today is to overcome all divisive and weakening tendencies by cultivating the nation, as an extended family, for living purpose and we can achieve this by at least three principles that Sardar Patel taught us:

First: Develop a national strategy with in-built flexibility and readiness in advance of the crises. There must not be any doubt or uncertainty where the national interest reposes. Whether it was the peasant protest in Gujarat to withhold land revenue from the British *Raj* in 1918, or at Bardoli in 1928, or the dynamic role in the Ahmedabad Municipality or the response to the accession problem of Junagarh and Hyderabad, Sardar Patel acted with national unity and national destiny in mind. He never accepted the agendas of narrow-minded groups at the cost of national interest. He stressed the vital need to achieve greater harmonization of India's national and federal interest with local and regional demands.

Second: Draw upon the total economic, social and political potential of the whole of India to meet the challenge of the modern world of intense competition. That is why he said in 1950:

"We pledged to work for complete independence. By God's grace we have redeemed that pledge; we need not to go into the many causes due to which we did not have to suffer as much for it as we might well have suffered...What has been achieved so far is like a peasant preparing the ground for cultivation. The true Swarajya has still to be created by us in India. Those who held up our work have left. There is no obstacle now. But millions in our country are

suffering today. They need food, clothing and shelter. At least there should be no lack of these things under self-rule... We should try to make our economy self-reliant."**

He rejected the idea that power should be given to small cliques or mafias who could monopolize decision-making. He had full faith in the democratic future of India and knew that people would create a society providing the greatest good for all, if they were given freedom and economic opportunity. The Sardar had full confidence that the great democratic traditions that are enshrined in the Indian Constitution would help in team building and communication with every segment of our society.

Third: He wanted all Indians to remember that India's future, whether in the context of security, prosperity or world leadership, was inextricably bound with "discipline". In a famous speech at Rajkot, after the victory at Bardoli before he became Congress President, he gave his candid assessment:

"You hope for much from me because a short while ago I was able to do something in Bardoli which you found inspiring and worthwhile. May I be frank? I do not like making public speeches: indeed I believe that too much talking does more harm

** Inaugurating an exhibition at Red Fort of Delhi on 29th January 1950, Sardar Patel expressed these views. He also said: "To ensure that food is available everywhere and no one starves, we have to import food grains. Arrangements have to be made to ensure at least subsistence ration everywhere, thus necessitating various control. These lead to many evils. In such a big country, it is not easy to have rationing and controls. The government is often brought into disrepute. People take bribes. Much else happens. But it is all our doing. Aliens have no hand in this. People blame the Government. To a certain extent they are right. But it also gives our people a bad name in the world-as people who cannot help each other at such a juncture, who cannot cooperate, cannot share. This is not good for us. It is not our way. If we want true Swarajya, we have to follow Mahatma Gandhi's way." [See appendix-c for details]

than good. I must tell you what is your principle defect; this I could do much better if I had the sweetness of tongue that you have. But I am a peasant and I have been accustomed to speak bluntly. I must therefore ask you to distinguish between politeness and flattery.... Our chief defect is lack of discipline."

There are many examples and sole-models to teach us how to organize our public life. India is rich in traditions, culture and contribution to universal civilization. But if we want to increase dedication and cooperation for meeting the challenges facing us today, Sardar Patel alone can help us to give our principles the greatest practical meaning. Sardar Patel's realism requires us to remain vigilant in this time of transition for India and the world.

4

SARDAR VALLABHBHAI PATEL: AN ICON OF THE ESSENCE OF *SHRIMAD BHAGVAD GITA*

Manoj Soni

"That there is today an India to think of and talk about is very largely due to Sardar Patel's statesmanship and firm administration." [-Babu Rajendra Prasad, Former President of India, May 1959].

These words brilliantly summarize the contribution of the great Sardar. Even the father of the Indian nation Mahatma Gandhi had acknowledged the contribution of Sardar Vallabhbhai Patel when he wrote that as an instrument of freedom struggle lies in the success of the Bardoli ***Satyagraha, "without the Sardar whatever has been accomplished could not have been possible"***. Indeed, the root of the success of the *Satyagraha* that adored Vallabhbhai with the beloved title of the "Sardar," N.V. Gadgil notes:

"From 1917 to 1947, what Gandhiji conceived, the Sardar concretized and carried out. It will be doing no injustice to Mahatmaji if it were to be

stated that this Satyagraha became acceptable to political India only after the success of Bardoli peasants in their Satyagraha of 1928." [Gadgil 1968].

While the last rites of the Sardar were being performed at Bombay, besides the pyre, C Rajagopalachari was heard saying to Dr. Rajendra Prasad:

"What inspiration, courage, confidence, and force incarnate Vallabhbhai was! We will not see the like of him again." [Nandurkar 1974].

Freedom Movement

The values of human dignity and freedom were nurtured into the personality of the Sardar right from his childhood. Even as a schoolboy, the Sardar is known to have shown extraordinary courage to fight against injustice.

While still a pupil of a school in his birth-town Nadiad, Vallabhbhai demonstrated his resolve of not relenting to the dictates of the powerful. Once it so happened in his class that, the teacher for a minor mischief heavily penalized a fellow student. That boy had no means to pay such a heavy penalty as imposed by the teacher ruthlessly. Next day as the student came to attend the school without being able to deposit the fine, the teacher asked him to leave the class and not attend the school until he would manage the fine money. Vallabhbhai found this behaviour of the teacher to be unjust. Someone else in place of Vallabhbhai, perhaps, could have offered to pay the fine money on behalf of the penalized fellow student. Instead, Vallabhbhai chose to root out the evil once and for all. He protested against the injustice meted out to the poor student and organized all the students with him. They resolved to support Vallabhbhai's stand and went on strike. Vallabhbhai's leadership qualities proved their worth and the Headmaster realized the significance of the cause for which Vallabhbhai had organized a successful strike. The Headmaster instructed the concerned teacher to withdraw the unjust punishment to the poor student and made sure that such ruthlessness is not repeated in future.

In another incident, Vallabhbhai was successful to prevent an immoral economic exploitation of his fellow students by another teacher of the same school. One of the teachers was found to compel the students of his school to purchase all the requisite stationery from him. He even used to exert subtle pressure on the helpless students against disobeying his instructions. When the matter came to light, Vallabhbhai got all the students united in boycotting the concerned teacher and not to buy from him under duress. Under the courageous leadership of Vallabhbhai, the students stopped buying from the concerned teacher, who understood the message and stopped trading goods while teaching in the school.

It was with the success of such significantly educative events in the early life of the Sardar that his personality nurtured the qualities of courage, determination and wisdom to defend the basic human values. And it was this very personality of Vallabhbhai that proved to be indomitable for the mighty British Empire. The British rulers in India got their first taste of the Sardar's leadership during the Kaira *Satyagraha* of 1917.

The Kaira *Satyagrah*

In 1917, Kaira district was challenged by the calamity of flood. The flood not only destroyed the entire ready-to-reap crop but proved disastrous for the Rabbi crop also. By well-established administrative norm, the government of the day was expected to postpone the collection of revenue on agriculture by one year. And that was what Shri Mohanlal Pandya, a social worker of Kathlal village urged the British rulers to do in his appeal. Instead of sympathizing with the calamity ravaged people of the district, and contrary to the norms and even basic humanitarian considerations the officials of the Kaira Collectorate ordered immediate collection of revenue from the peasants who had their entire Crop either destroyed due to flood or failed due to its after-effects.

Mohanlalji appealed Gandhiji to come to the rescue of the poor peasants of the Kaira district. Gandhiji was convinced of the inhuman and unjust administrative action on the part of the Kaira Collectorate. But, true to his style, prior to launching a mass struggle based on the principles of *Satyagraha*, Gandhiji tried to negotiate with the concerned officials to reconsider their stand. The government did not give in and order forceful seizure of property of those who failed to deposit their revenue to the government. Finally, in his last attempt to negotiate an amicable settlement, Gandhiji wrote to the Commissioner on 20th March 1918 to postpone the collection of revenue for one year. The reply was as expected. The government refused to budge. And thus was launched the first mass scale *Satyagraha* movement against the British rule in Kaira on 22nd March 1918. On that day a huge gathering of peasants of Kaira assembled in Nadiad, and took oath of abiding by the principles of *Satyagraha* in their fight against the British injustice and inhuman administration with regard to the collection of revenue in an agriculturally failed year. Vallabhbhai, who not only gave up his lucrative legal practice, but, also his aristocratic life-style and plunged into the Gandhiji-led struggle with complete devotion and unflinching conviction, willingly shouldered the responsibility of steering the movement.

It was during this *Satyagraha* that the qualities of Vallabhbhai's leadership began translating the otherwise difficult-to-sustain movement into a vibrant mass agitation of a unique kind. The government's offensive actions started getting crueler as each day passed, but

Vallabhbhai's leadership ensured that the peasants stayed united in their resolve to fight the untruth with the non-violent weapon of *Satyagraha*. His words ignited the fire of patriotism in the hearts of the peasants and his devotion inspired unshakable resolve in the minds of even those who had to suffer heavily the brunt of the British administration. Said he:

"This struggle will put the whole nation on fire. No joy can ever be found without the experience of pain, and if it is found it cannot be sustained. The people with firm resolve are the true merit of a nation. A coward people's nation is disgraceful. And Kaira is the land of brave hearts in India..." [Klarthi 1975].

And it did happen as Vallabhbhai had foreseen. The Kaira *Satyagraha* was hailed by the whole nation by scores of messages of solidarity. At one instance, even the Collector was impressed by the non-violent, peaceful and tolerant approach of the *Satyagrahi* struggle.

At last, the government had to backtrack. On 6th June 1918, the legitimate and just demands of the peasants were granted and the struggle came to a successful end only to begin on still larger scale against the British injustices and atrocities in Nagpur's flag-hoisting *Satyagraha*, Borsad's "*haidiya*" tax collection, Bardoli's unjustified enhanced revenue collection and finally across the whole of Indian sub-continent. But, the significance of Kaira *Satyagraha* lies in the fact that Gandhiji had convincingly found his most brilliant lieutenant Vallabhbhai, who was destined to be the Sardar of the heart and mind of India and her citizens for all time to come.

The Bardoli *Satyagrah*

If the Kaira *Satyagraha* proved the mettle of Vallabhbhai, it was the Bardoli *Satyagraha* that crowned him with the title of the "Sardar". In 1921, Bardoli was identified by the Mahatma as the focal point of launching the nationwide movement of non-cooperation with the British government. Consequently, the British rulers attempted a pre-emptive strike of terrorizing the local people of Bardoli by enhancing the revenue by a whopping 22 per cent, without any justifiable cause.

With the consent of Gandhiji and with the active co-operation of Darbar Gopaldas, Ravishankar Maharaj, Dr Chandubhai Desai, Abbas Saheb Taiyabji, Gordhandas Chokhawala, Dr Sumant Mehta, Imam Saheb, Shardaben Mehta, Kalyanjibhai Mehta, Kunwarjibhai, Jugatrambhai Dave, Khushalbhai, Narharibhai, Tribhovandasbhai and local Patel leaders of Bardoli, Vallabhbhai took charge of the peasants struggle for convincing the government of the day to roll back the unjustified revenue enhancement. Vallabhbhai, in spite of the unjustified pre-emptive coercion by the local British administration, urged the government to at least postpone the collection of the enhanced revenue collection till an independent inquiry is made in to the justification of the enhancement in the revenue. While he assured the administration that the peasants would pay their due revenue at the prevailing rate immediately, in case the administration agreed to postpone the collection of the enhanced revenue till the report of the independent inquiry arrived; he also warned them that, given the adamant attitude of the administration, the peasants would launch *Satyagraha* and defer paying even their due revenue to the government in protest. He even dared the government to take any punitive action that it thought appropriate against the peasants who were resolutely united to face harshest consequences of their just struggle through a unique means of *Satyagraha* under the leadership of Vallabhbhai.

The British government did not budge and failed to gauge the morale of the peasants in Bardoli. The

Satyagraha was thus launched in February 1928. Few could have foreseen it to be a movement that was destined to mark a turning point in the Indian freedom struggle. And it proved to be that milestone, indeed.

The Bardoli *Satyagraha* brought out the strategist in Vallabhbhai. He could very well identify the weak links in the movement and strengthened them with the power of his wise and courageous words. Thus, he strengthened the morale of the womenfolk who were prone to succumb when the British administration started confiscating peasants property including and especially the livestock. To the womenfolk of the area Vallabhbhai said:

'I ask the women whether they got married to their livestock. You are married to brave peasants. Should there arise a need to abandon the Taluka or even the whole state, be prepared to do so; but, make sure that your pledge and prestige remain intact.' [Translated from Klarthi 1975].

Vallabhbhai's words had their effect on the morale of the womenfolk who became further resolute to support the struggle of *Satyagraha* against the British administration's injustice. And to the other weak link, the Patel of the village who was the serving agent of the administration, Vallabhbhai addressed using sharp satire:

'Government's vehicle in the villages runs on the two bullocks, viz., the Patel and the Talati. They have to tolerate the whip of their Master, but are happy since they are sometime offered a piece of jiggery. Patels, you must learn the real Patelship, and tell the Collector not to include your name in the list of slaves. Tell him that you would not like to feast upon such black deeds.' [Translated from Klarthi 1975].

The Patels too realized the spirit of Vallabhbhai's laser sharp words and stepped down by offering their resignations to their respective British authorities. But, the real challenge was to sustain and strengthen the *Satyagrahi* fighting spirit of a heterogeneous population of Bardoli *Taluka*.

Half of the Taluka's 87,000 population consisted of *Dublas* and Tribals; a third were *Patidars*; Muslims and *Anavil Brahmins* were four per cent each; while, Banias and untouchables formed two per cent each. In the initial phase of the struggle mostly the *Patidars* out of the Landholding communities of *Brahmins*, *Banias*, Muslims and *Parsis* offered their strong support to the movement. About the rest grave apprehensions prevailed. To those sitting on the fence, Sardar sent a strong message of courage and patriotic sentiments in one of his speeches:

"I know some of you are afraid of your lands being confiscated. Will they take the lands away to England? The worst that can happen is that the lands might be transferred to Government in their books, but if you are united you can defy anyone to come forward to cultivate those lands. Government has at the most one headman and one Talati to every village, while we have every adult in the village." [Desai 1957].

The fire in the words, reason, conviction and resolve of Vallabhbhai had magical effect in boosting the morale of even those who had never even dreamt of a life free of the British domination. And right from the very beginning of the *Satyagraha* in Bardoli, Vallabhbhai made it amply clear to the peasants and the land holders that it was, after all, *their* struggle not his alone:

"I still ask you to think twice before you take the plunge. Do not take comfort from the feeling that you have as your leader a fighter like me. Forget me and forget my companions, fight if you feel that you must resist oppression and injustice. If you

miserably fail, you will not rise again for several years, but if you succeed you will have done much to lay the foundations of SWARAJ". [Desai 1957].

So great was the penetrative clarity and brevity of Vallabhbhai's Gujarati language in his speeches in Bardoli that Mahadevbhai's Desai once remarked, "Never before have I heard such brilliance in his language. While Narhari Parikh noted, "It is from the speeches of Vallabhbhai in Bardoli that the lovers of Gujarati discovered how rich their language was." Consider the following incident to gauge the impact of Vallabhbhai's fiery words in raising the national spirit of the people in Bardoli.

Bhavanbhai Hirabhai Patel of the Nani Farod village was charged with the offence of injuring the officer when he had come to confiscate his property. In fact, it was his wife who had, banged the door of their house on the officer, when Bhavanbhai was not even present in the house. Yet the police chose to punish Bhavanbhai instead of his wife. Before his trial, Bhavanbhai's wife brought him to Vallabhbhai in the Swaraj Ashram and said to her husband, 'look, no faltering timid words before the magistrate! Ask him to punish you as severely as he wishes. Do not be bothered about our children and me. Retort in manly accent.' Then she turned to Vallabhbhai and shared her disappointment, 'What a pity they did not prosecute me!' Bhavanbhai was sentenced to six months prison. The lady once again tried to put courage in her husband's heart. Said she, ***'Go to jail bravely - without worrying about our children or me. May God give you strength and courage?'*** This is not the end of the story, for it involved more than mere words of patriotic feelings; it involved real dedication to the Cause of *Swaraj.* After her husband was taken away, the lady came to the *Swaraj Ashram* and offered to Vallabhbhai nine rupees, the family's total savings, for use in *Satyagraha* at Bardoli! [Gandhi 1999].

The Bardoli struggle was also an occasion that provided the humble peasants of the district an important lesson in realizing their self-confidence and their inner strength. Vallabhbhai's inspiring words were like the magic wand that unravelled the power that lay untapped in the united front that the peasants had put up before the British *Raj*. Said the Sardar, while witnessing the unabated confiscation of not just the peasants' livestock and property, but also the livestock of the Washer men or tailors who did not own an inch of land and hence had no tax due to the *Raj*:

"Government has run amuck. It thinks it can trample everything under its feet. Even so thinks the mad elephant, priding itself on having trampled even lions and tigers to death, and scorning the little gnat defying him. I am teaching the little gnat today to let the elephant go on in his mad career and then get into his trunk at the opportune moment". [Desai 1970, p.63].

It was due to the unmatched brilliance and indomitable courage of the leadership of Vallabhbhai that someone in Bardoli referred to him as "SARDAR", sometimes in April 1928, in the most natural way. And the title was readily and swiftly popularized as everyone who came in his magnetic touch could immediately relate the meaning of the title with the personality of Vallabhbhai. Gandhiji too adopted the peasants' appellation as he wrote in one of his letters to Vallabhbhai during the Bardoli *Satyagraha*, ***" ...long live the Sardar to fight many a good fight... the battle in Bardoli is going very well..."***[Gandhi 1957, p.9].

Banias, Muslims, Parsis and Tribals joined the *Patidars* in this struggle as the dislike for the tax and disgust of the methods of the *Raj* transformed them into a wall of opposition to the British injustices. *Banias* did not yield even when their land was confiscated and their sons arrested for obstructing the confiscation. Neither did the Tribals yield even when they were deprived of their only sources of livelihood. Muslims were inspired and encouraged by the Imam and Abbas Taiyabji to sign the *Satyagraha* pledge, while the Maulanas' *Fatwa* strengthened the resolve of the community not to purchase the seized property from the government. In short, the whole population rose in a unified fashion against the unjust and cruel British administration in Bardoli.

Finally, the *Raj* was compelled to yield. The first amongst the Government's arm of establishment to concede the ascendancy of the Sardar in the conflict was the *Times of India*. After touring Bardoli *Taluka* its correspondence found that Vallabhbhai had ***"instituted a Bolshevik regime";*** and that the *Raj*'s writ had ceased to run in the *Taluka* but that of the Sardar did. The correspondent also reported the ***"iron discipline prevailing in Bardoli",*** the devotion of the peasants to Vallabhbhai, and the resignation of eighty headmen and nineteen *Talatis*. ***"The subordinate officers are at the mercy of the Satyagraha commander",*** reported the correspondent [Times of India, 3.7.28].

The Vallabhbhai-Wilson [the then Governor of Bombay – Sir Leslie Wilson] meeting in Surat and exertions of intermediaries, of whom Kanaiyalal Munshi was one, had indicated that while the Government was prepared to reconsider the assessment of the revenue, release the prisoners, reinstate the public servants who had resigned and even return the confiscated property not yet sold, it was not willing to arrange the restoration of the land that had already been sold. The Sardar was not prepared to settle for any compromise that did not include complete restoration of all the seized property by the Government. He was also opposed to the idea of an advance deposit of the new revenue by the peasants who were to refund their due if the new assessment was to be reversed.

Finally, the Sardar triumphed. Following the tough negotiation between Vallabhbhai and Sir Chunilal Mehta, a Finance Member of the Bombay Government, all the obstacles to the settlement of the dispute were removed. Thus, annulling its earlier threat, while the Government agreed to buy back the sold property and restore the same to its original owner, the advance deposit tangle was solved by the ingenuity of Vithalbhai, who induced Ramchandra Bhatt, a Bombay-based businessman from Bardoli *Taluka*, to deposit the difference amount between the old and the new revenue assessment.

While Vallabhbhai agreed to the restoration of the property procedure, he had serious objection to the deposit idea by Mr. Bhatt. But, Mahadevbhai's logic that condoning Mr. Bhatt's offer was not same as conceding the demand of the *Raj*, since neither Vallabhbhai nor the peasants had agreed to deposit the sum with the Government, helped Vallabhbhai to reluctantly accept the arrangement.

The significance of the success of the Bardoli *Satyagraha* lays not so much in getting the unjust policy of the British reversed as in proving the efficacy of *Satyagraha* as a novel weapon of political resistance to an unjust regime. This was indicated in a private reappraisal of Sir Leslie Wilson, the then Governor of Bombay, who is on record to have admitted that, **"the Government has no effective weapon in dealing with Satyagraha"**. [Letter of 16.8.28, in File 197 of 1928, Home Political, National Archives, New Delhi].

It is quite common of human tendency to expect personal benefits in whatever form out of even the smallest sacrifice made for others in society. But, the Sardar was an exception. He dedicated his entire life and all his abilities to the freedom struggle for India and accepted the Mahatma and his word without any condition or question. That he was unceremoniously surpassed to install Jawaharlal as the first Prime Minister of India happened much later; even as early as in 1929, he generously made way for Jawaharlal to assume the Presidency of the Congress, in spite of being supported by more number of PCCs compared to Jawaharlal. The following is only one of the many instances when Vallabhbhai chose not to claim his due but to serve India and her people as a devotee. It speaks a lot about the character of the Sardar and brings out his commitment for harmony within the team of the Congress under the leadership of the Mahatma.

A successor to Motilal Nehru was to be chosen to preside over the Congress in 1929. As Subhas Chandra Bose has noted:

"The general feeling in the Congress circle was that the honour should go to Sardar Vallabhbhai Patel". [Bose, 1964, p.169].

However, a number of Congressmen, including Vallabhbhai, felt that Gandhiji himself would be the best choice to lead the freedom struggle as he had conceived it in its key phase. The Mahatma however declined to take over. Thus, Vallabhbhai, who was backed by five PCCs, compared to three who backed Jawaharlal was the natural democratic choice for the Congress presidency. Two young and enthusiastic supporters of Jawaharlal from U.P., Narendra Dev and B K Sharma, doubted the abilities of the Sardar by asking, ***"What is the Sardar going to do [as the Congress President]?"*** [Gandhi, 1999, p.181] Vallabhbhai withdrew his name immediately on Gandhi's asking, and never nurtured any grudge, nor even expressed his hurt that would have been caused, for several understandable reasons.

To begin with the 1929-30 Congress was meant to be a turning point in India's freedom struggle, as it turned out to be, and thus was expected to possibly project Gandhi's successor. Secondly, Jawaharlal was a much younger man than the Sardar, and to yield to a younger leader would not come naturally to a *Charottar Patidar*. Thirdly, the Sardar was himself not convinced of the abilities of Jawaharlal to make a better President than himself. Finally, and the most importantly, adding injury to the insult by the importunity of the likes of *Devs* and *Sharmas*, the Sardar was perceived to be found wanting by none other than Gandhi – a man for whose sake the Sardar had given up home and hearth. In the September 1929 issue of the *Young India*, while acknowledging the significance of the Bardoli *Satyagraha* and the Sardar's abilities, Gandhiji, seems to assign greater credit to the environment of the Bardoli than to the ability of the man who created and nurtured it. Sprinkling apprehension on the Sardar's leadership abilities, Gandhi remarked:

"But he [the Sardar] needs a Bardoli to make good his leadership. How many Bardolis are there ready in the country today?" [Young India, 5.9.1929].

The treatment to the Sardar was, thus, bitter. But, he nipped all hurt in the bud and remained a loyal soldier of the freedom movement till his last breath. One thing, as Rajmohan Gandhi has noted in his brilliant study of the Sardar's life, was very clear to Gandhi, Nehru and everybody; and that was that:

"In Gujarat only [Sardar] Patel's writ would run, not the Congress President's, not even the Mahatma's... his [the Sardar's] hand would remain free in Gujarat" [Gandhi, 1999, p.182].

Summing up the Gandhi-Sardar relationship, Kishorlal Mashruwala has very well captured the essential character: ***"I would describe the Gandhi-Patel***

relationship as that of brothers, Gandhi being the senior brother, and Gandhi-Nehru as that of father and son". [Mashruwala, 1983, p.148].

References

Gadgil, N. V., 1968, *Government from Inside*, Meerut, Meenakshi Publication.

Nandurkar, G. M. [Edited], Patel Manibehn Vallabhbhai [Co-Ord. Ed.], 1974, This was Sardar-The Commemorative Volume, Volume I, Ahmedabad, Sardar Vallabhbhai Smarak Bhavan.

Klarthi, Mukulbhai, 1975, *Satyagrahi Sardar,* Ahmedabad, Navajivan Prakashan Mandir

Desai, Mahadev, 1957, *The Story of Bardoli*, Ahmedabad, Navajivan Publishing House.

Desai, Ishwarlal [Edited], 1970, *Bardoli Satyagraha*, Surat

Gandhi, M.K., 1957, *Letters to Sardar Patel*, Ahmedabad, Navajivan Prakashan Mandir

Bose, Subhas Chandra, 1964, *The Indian Struggle*, Bombay, Asia Publishing House.

Gandhi, Rajmohan, 1999, Patel: A Life, Ahmedabad, Navajivan Publishing House.

Kumar, Ravindra, 1991, Life and Work of Sardar Vallabhbhai Patel, New Delhi, Atlantic Publishers and Distributors

5

Sardar Vallabhbhai Patel: A Man of Multidimensional Personality

B. J. Patel

Life and work of Sardar Vallabhbhai Patel is an account of a humble peasant's child, somehow making his way to barristership and plunging headlong in the struggle for freeing his motherland. He was an example of a person of iron will, courage of conviction, God fearing, truthful, painstaking, determined, selfless service overcoming social, political and economic hurdles, who rose to the pinnacle of glory through qualities of head and heart and relentless efforts.

Sardar's contribution in vindicating Gandhiji's ideals of truthfulness and non-violence and establishing the eleven vows that Gandhiji swore by, were not mere empty words or slogans but everyone thereof could be put in practice is brought out in this thesis. Prior to Gandhiji's coming on the political horizon, nowhere in the world it was imagined that an emasculated country could offer a brave non-violent resistance to a mighty empire. Sardar repeatedly established the efficacy of non-violent non-co-operation and passive resistance, through Kaira [1918], Nagpur [1923], Borsad [1923-24] and Bardoli *Satyagrahas* [1928], each of which was conducted with mottos of unity, discipline, truthfulness, non-violence, ethical behaviour, religious tolerance, far sighted strategy and determined leadership. Sardar undertook leadership in farmers' struggles after preparing them for a determined struggle entailing highest sacrifice to be offered cheerfully and without venom, malice or hatred. He succeeded substantially in all the struggles judged from the points of view of fidelity to ideology and achievement of the goal. These successes inspired the country to face the Civil Disobedience Movement, popularly known as the *Salt Satyagraha* [1930], Individual *Satyagraha* [1940] and also the Quit India Movement 1942].

Sardar's leadership in various struggles and experience of running the Ahmedabad Municipal administration prepared him to meet peace time challenges like cholera in Ahmedabad, excessive rains in several parts of Gujarat including Ahmedabad itself and Borsad plague, all of which he faced successfully with courage, determination and strenuous work evoking enthusiastic popular support.

His tactful and courageous handling of municipal affairs, later on shaped him to meet greater challenges of free India in the shape of exodus of millions of refugees, communal hatred, lawlessness, unprecedented violence, setting up of services afresh, shortage of food grains due to substantial production going to Pakistan, unification of States, division of assets and liabilities between the new countries, framing of the new Constitution, headaches of Kashmir and Hyderabad and also of Junagarh, at the age of 72 with several physical ailments.

Sardars life is a fascinating story of all these challenges and how they are met by this loyal soldier of Gandhiji and Pandit Jawaharlal Nehru successfully achieving many laurels and establishing himself sometimes as superior to Bismarck, Machiavelli, Napoleon, Lenin, Mao Tse-Tung and Chanakya and yet humbly passing on the credit to Gandhiji, Pandit Jawaharlal Nehru, or the brave peasantry, himself being only the instrument or tool as per the Divine Will.

The secret of his successes in struggles is his identification with the cause, readiness to be in the vanguard, selflessness, devotion to duty, brotherly feelings for colleagues and co-workers, meticulous planning, discipline, inspiring simplicity, hardihood, truthfulness, courage and principle approach.

Administrative achievements of Sardar Vallabhbhai Patel are largely due to his close study of problems, liberal treatment of subordinates, catholicity of outlook, faith in the services, inspiring leadership for meeting challenges, impartiality, selflessness, non-interference, disciplines and hard work.

Unification of the country was achieved by conciliatory approach, appeal to the patriotism of the rulers, appreciation of their sacrifice, liberal acknowledgement of their contributions, presentation of hard realities of going alone and minimum force where inevitable, venomlessness and progressing step by step – beginning with stand still agreement and ultimately leading to merger.

Success in maintaining law and order was achieved by impartiality, sympathetic consideration about the predicament of Muslims in India, sympathetic handling of the refugee problem and ruthless suppression of lawlessness.

Sardar played an important role in the drafting of the Constitution also as the head of the sub-committees on minorities, fundamental rights and centre state relationship, in each of which his cool headedness and power of persuasion was effective.

He was a faithful follower of Mahatma Gandhi, but was able to persuade Gandhiji to his point of view as in the case of partition or to permit himself to go his own way as in the case of his desire to assist the war efforts if freedom was guaranteed after the war. Similarly he did not agree with Pandit Jawaharlal Nehru in putting up Rajaji[1] as the first President of India instead of Rajendra Babu and not agreeing with Pandit Jawaharlal in opposing Tandonji's[2] candidature for Congress Presidency, on both occasions Pandit Jawaharlal Nehru wanting to resign but being persuaded by Sardar to be amiable to the democratic procedure of accepting the majority verdict.

He had clear approach regarding the untouchability problem. He stressed on prohibition, opposed child marriage, advocated widow remarriage, independence of women from economic subservience and desired for educational reforms. Also he stressed on basic education, mother tongue as the medium of instruction and supported whole-heatedly the proposal to accept Hindi as *Rashtra Bhasha*; he stressed on technical training, desired for self sufficiency in food grains, decentralization of industries, and opposed indiscriminate nationalization.

Sardar Patel life gives us a fair idea of the stature, character and calibre of a humble son of India who successfully scaled great heights through self help, dedication and relentless struggle with a self effacing approach.

References

1. C. Rajagopalachari.
2. Purushottam Das Tandon.

6

The Economic Ideas of Sardar Patel

Raj Kumar Kothari

Sardar Vallabhbhai Patel, the 'Iron Man of India', was an indomitable freedom fighter, a strong administrator and a devout patriot. He was a realist and a man of action who did not have faith in any specific ideology. A man of tremendous patience & absolute simplicity, Sardar Patel was a great leader in the cause of independence. His achievements as a statesman, administrator and politician are incomparable. A closer examination to some of his correspondence shows that Sardar Patel had a very pragmatic approach towards Indian economy and his contributions in this field are seminal.

Sardar Patel did not recognize the role of any specific theory of planned economic structure or development. Even though a close follower of Gandhi, Patel did not accept in practice even the basic principles of Gandhian economy. He did not prescribe an agricultural based economy for India. Rather he underscored the need for rapid industrial development. Patel never supported the case for development of cottage industries as preached by Gandhi and thus represented different views on industrialization.

Sardar Patel did not approve the general means to achieve the goal of industrial socialism. He opposed nationalized industrial system of the socialist pattern and did not favour the introduction of such a system in India at that time. He believed that theoretical socialism of the Marxist type with its roots in the context of the European civilization of the West could not be suited to India. He disparaged the usefulness of adopting socialist ideas to Indian social and economic structure. The history of India and her political and economic development had been different from what operated in the Western countries. In India, Patel wanted that socialism should be developed on a cooperative basis rather than imposed by the state. He disagreed with Nehru on the road to bring about economic and social changes by coercion. He accepted Gandhian socialism in a modified form. However, despite having differences with Gandhi and Nehru on the road to economic development, Patel always admired them. This reflects his magnificent personality, a rare phenomenon in politics.

Sardar Patel expressed his displeasure over Nehruvian model of economic development. In the post-independence period, the Indian National Congress accepted the ideal of a "socialistic pattern of society". The socialistic pattern connotes social ownership or state control of the principal means of production and the equitable distribution of resources of the nation. In Nehru's scheme, the public sector in the field of heavy and basic industries was to be the dominant force for the economic advance of the country. Patel in contrast suggested that public and private sectors, both, could play equally important and meaningful role in the economic planning and development of the country. Only the central and state governments would not be in a position to control and run industries efficiently. He opposed large-scale nationalization of industries and thus recognized the importance of private enterprise in key areas of the economy. Patel refused to subscribe the view that all private property and profits were immoral. According to him, profits within reasonable limits should be recognized to enable the industrialists to expand their production base. Patel, in fact, pleaded for more balanced adjustments between public and private sectors for national economic development. Thus his policies were directed towards making the country industrially strong and economically viable. At the same time, Sardar Patel had faith upon socialist ideas and principles although in a modified form. With regard to the socialists, he stated that once India was free & highly industrialized they [the socialists] could attempt to convert the country into a socialist state. Patel, however, did not believe expropriation of the Landlords' and *Zamindars*' would help the landless. The Socialists with Nehru's support advocated the policy of taking over land from big landlords and giving it to peasants - Patel vehemently opposed this move.

Sardar Patel's approach to contemporary Indian economy was dictated by two key propositions: first, Patel did not prescribe any specific ideology for economic development and second, he believed in creating strong economic foundation through hard work, sacrifice and devotion. He believed in national consolidation and therefore advocated the necessity of increasing the social efficiency and enhancing the moral character of the people as prerequisites for national growth.

For the sake of industrial advancement, Patel wanted to forge unity among labour, capital and government. He believed that all three had common outlook. Any step in the direction of economic development must be taken after mutual consultation among them. According to him, conflict among the three would be ruinous to the country and a big blow to India's industrial future. He wanted that the Indian economy should develop in such a way so that the vast number of inhabitants could be provided with gainful employment, rather than being displaced by the large-scale introduction of machines. According to him only a cooperative system could mobilize the vast manpower of the country.

Patel advocated industrial peace in which violent method advocated by the Communists had no place. He believed in the promotion of free enterprises and stated that the industrialists should concentrate on getting maximum, out of their plants and machinery and labour, should extend their helping hand to the industrialists to exploit their resources to the maximum national advantage. Thus, Patel wanted to establish Indian economy through rapid industrialization. In fact, he did not believe in rural and urban economy or agricultural or industrial economy as two ways for the national economic development. He took both of them as interrelated to each other. Patel, however, favoured industrialization because he believed that without it rural and agricultural development could not be possible.

Keeping in mind national interests of the country, Patel introduced a Bill in the Constituent Assembly, which provided for the prevention of strikes in certain essential services. Strong opposition came from the pro-left Congress quarters, especially the Socialists. Yielding under pressure, Nehru withdrew the Bill despite being opposed by Patel. Patel held the view that what labour was entitled to must be settled satisfactorily and peacefully. But for that the correct method was not stoppage of work nor sabotage but arbitration. Further, he stated that production was the key to progress and thus stoppage of work constituted an act of disservice to the country. He therefore wanted to determine labour wages in proportion to production.

Patel however believed in the principles of economic equality and stated that after industrial development- the policy of equitable distribution of resources could be implemented. In this way Patel sympathized with the cause of labour. He asked the industrialists to understand that labour was the driving force for the stabilization of India's freedom and that no government could afford to ignore what should be due to them.

One and the only objective of the state, according to Patel, was to stimulate economic growth with support from all corners - industrialists, workers or the common public. Patel thus did not share the Marxist view that the 'state is an instrument of economic exploitation'. He believed that the capitalist and worker both have an important role to play in the process of economic development. Patel thus did not pay much attention toward class division in the society. He also did not agree with the Marxist thinkers that the state promotes inequality & uneven distribution of resources in the society. It would, however, be wrong to brand him as pro-capitalist since his policies were not directed against interests of the workers.

Critics however branded Patel as rightist, conservative and anti-socialist due to his personal friendship with some capitalists and the rulers of the princely states. The socialist branded him as a friend only of the capitalists because he was against the use of weapons of strikes in the industries. Ramesh Thapar held the view that Patel always stood for the interests of the dominant class only. He further stated that slogans rose by Patel about progress and economic equality were part of his election propaganda only. P. G. Mavalankar, however, commented that Patel was neither against socialism or communism, nor he was a conservative or rightist. Manibehn rightly pointed out that despite being close to the capitalists, Patel never meant to support them. He did not amass personal wealth for himself. Besides, he stood by the labour against the mill-owners in the Ahmedabad Mills strike in 1917. He made a crusade against landowners in favour of the *Adivasis* who were made serfs by them in Surat district.

Sardar Patel was a man of action and did not have much time to engage in speculation of abstract ideas and thinking. Patel's economic thinking was thus simple, co-coordinated, non-ideological applicable in equitable measures as much to labour and the poor as to the capitalists. He was neither an ideologue, nor a slave to the capitalists. Dorothy Norman discovered in him a gentle person, a man of great simplicity without but one thought - the well being of the future India. Though he is regarded as the '*Iron Man of India*', Sardar Patel was intensely humane, fair minded, magnanimous and self-sacrificing. Despite having differences of thought, temperament and style, he stood by Gandhi and Nehru in the hours of crises in the greater interest of the country and its people.

References

1. Das, Durga [ed.], Sardar Patel's Correspondence: 1945-50, 10 Volumes, Ahmedabad: Navajivan Publishing House, 1971.
2. Sen, S. P. [ed.], Dictionary of National Biography, Volume III, Calcutta: Institute of Historical Studies, 1974.

Newspapers and Magazines

1. Bombay Chronicle.
2. Harijan.
3. Statesman.
4. Young India.

Secondary Sources

1. Ahluwalia, B.K., Sardar Patel: A Life, New Delhi: Sagar Publications, 1974.
2. Bakshi, S.R., Sardar Patel: His Political Ideology, New Delhi: Anmol Publications, 1990.
3. Gandhi, Rajmohan, Patel: A Life, Ahmedabad: Navajivan Publishing House, 1991.

4. Krishna, B., Sardar Vallabhbhai Patel: India's Iron Man, New Delhi: INDUS, 1995.
5. Kumar, Ravindra, Life and Work of Sardar Vallabhbhai Patel, New Delhi: Atlantic Publishers, 1991.
6. Parikh, Narhari, Sardar Vallabhbhai Patel, Vol. 2, Ahmedabad: Navajivan, 1971.
7. Pathak, D., & Seth, P., Sardar Patel: From Civic to National Leadership, Ahmedabad: Navajivan, 1980.
8. Sarin, L. N., Sardar Patel, New Delhi: S. Chand, 1972.
9. Tahmankar, D. V., Sardar Patel, London: George Allen & Unwin, 1970.

7

We Could Say Patel was The Best Prime Minister

J.N. Chaturvedi

When India became independent, I was a university student. Yet, till then I had never seen Sardar Patel except in pictures. The first time I had a close view of him was when, after Gandhiji's assassination, his ashes were brought to Allahabad for immersion at the *Sangam*. He sat unmoved on the top of the cortege with a sad, pensive look throughout his journey of five km to the *Sangam*. The next time, was in 1948 when he addressed the University convocation at which I received my bachelor's degree. The address was direct and in matter of fact, free from any rhetoric.

About the time I was awaiting the result of the Civil Services examination, he, the architect of the two All India Services, the I. A. S. and the I. P. S. as one of the pillars of national integration, lay ill and, to the misfortune of this country, passed away on the 15th December 1950.

A real and rather fortuitous addition to my peripheral knowledge of that great personality came only in February 1952. H. V. R. Ayyangar, who was then the Union Home

Secretary, was, on his annual visit to the Central Police Training College [later renamed Sardar Vallabhbhai Patel National Police Academy**] where I was under training as an I.P.S. probationer.

At the mess dinner, Ayyangar reminisced about his long association with the late Sardar, the country's first Home Minister. Amongst the several experiences which he narrated, was the one relating to a Congress Working Committee [C.W.C.] Resolution asking the Central Government to create a new state of Andhra Pradesh in line with their commitment of carving out linguistic states whenever they assumed power? The Sardar as the Home Minister who endorsed that to Ayyangar for comments received a copy of the C.W.C. Resolution. Ayyangar took that to the Sardar ***"Sir"***, Ayyangar told him, ***"This is virtually a decision of the government. What am I supposed to comment on?"***

The Sardar looked at him sternly and replied, ***"Are you the country's Home Secretary or are you not?" "Of course I am"***, Ayyangar replied. ***"Then"***, said the Sardar, ***"Do your duty."***

Ayyangar went back and recorded a detailed note demolishing the case for linguistic states as totally inopportune and highly detrimental to process of national integration. ***"It was"***, Ayyangar told us, ***"a tribute to the open mindedness and sagacity of Sardar Patel that a repletion, to which he was himself a party as a member of the Congress Working Committee, was rejected by him as the country's Home Minister."*** The message, that the services ought to function totally fearlessly and apolitically, was loud and clear in this single decision.

It is a pity that the successors of both, Sardar Patel, as well as, Ayyangar so soon lost their way. And, it is

**At Hyderabad.

thus, that the Manchester Guardian [now the Guardian] wrote in its obituary on Patel, ***"The same man is seldom successful both as rebel and statesman. Patel was the exception."***

Unlike many others, Patel brushed aside the question, ***"After you who?"*** in a manner characteristic of him. His reply was, ***"The cemeteries of the world are full of indispensable people."*** Tanya Zink in, a British Journalist chose to reproduce this memorable quote on the cover of her book ***"CHALLENGES OF INDIA."***

As many Britons said of Richard Butler, we could say, ***"Patel was the best Prime Minister India ever had."***

8

The Economic Ideas of Sardar Patel and Their Relevance Today

Amit Dholakia

Introduction

Sardar Vallabhbhai Patel [1875-1950] - a key figure of the Indian National Movement, leader of several mass struggles and builder of the Congress party has earned his place in history as one of the foremost statesmen and makers of modern India. His historic and astounding role in the seemingly impossible integration of India's more than 570 princely states is well-known and well-documented. As the principal architect of the constitution of India and builder of the *'steel frame'* of Indian bureaucracy, the Sardar's contributions are far-reaching and fundamental to Indian political system. However, as Nani Palkhivala says:

"The nation has not realized the greatness of Vallabhbhai as it should have done. If Vallabhbhai had not lived India would not be what it is... Our greatest tragedy is that the lessons taught by this

***outstanding Indian patriot and statesman who unquestioningly ranks in the world class, are so little remembered today."*[1]**

Even as the Sardar's other contributions have been written about, most people are not well-acquainted with his approach to India's economic problems and their solution. This paper, therefore, attempts to present and assess Sardar Patel's economic views and ascertain their relevance in the contemporary times.

The Sardar was a man of action than of words. He believed in doing things rather than giving long discourses or writing about them at length. He had neither time nor inclination for serious intellectual reflection on economic theories and models of development. His economic vision was, therefore, shaped by his robust and unfailing common sense and rich experience of grassroots mobilization. It was marked by flexibility and apathy for ideological rigidity. The Sardar did not value such theories or economic principles that cannot be implemented for the benefit of the common masses. His considered reflections on the economic problems that arose after independence and his responses to the policies suggested by other leaders of the Congress Party, especially by the socialist leaders, as well as the speeches delivered by him on the making of India's economic policy offer insights about his economic vision.

Ideas on Agriculture and Rural India

Inspired by Mahatma Gandhi, Sardar Patel believed that tens of thousands of villages are the soul of India. Unless the fruits of economic development and social progress reach the rural people and their standard of living is uplifted, there could be no real turn-around in India's position. Agriculture is the mainstay of rural economic and social life. The majority of the Indian people depend upon agriculture for their survival and employment. For centuries, it has influenced the culture, value systems and thoughts of the Indians. The Sardar considered farmers to be the main drivers of the Indian economy and engines of its growth. Though he was a foreign-educated barrister, he took pride in calling himself an agriculturist in view of his family profession and background. He always used to remind the farmers that as producers of food for the people, they should never feel powerless or dependent upon others. He was deeply perturbed by the prevalence of poverty, exploitation, malnutrition, starvation, illiteracy and disease among the rural people and felt that unity among farmers was vital for solving these problems. He, therefore, wanted the improvement and growth of agriculture to be given top priority in the plans for economic development. India experienced recurrent crisis in food security at the time of independence. Import of food grains was a burden on foreign exchange reserves and scarce national resources. Hence, the Sardar emphasized self-sufficiency in food and production of more food grains as items of high priority.

Ideas on Industry and Industrialists

Sardar Patel also recognized the need for rapid industrial growth for the generation of employment and prosperity in the country. He felt that the private industrialists and capitalists who had the requisite experience and entrepreneurial spirit were best suited to take rapid stride in the direction of industrialization. He felt that the government had neither the resources nor the competence to set up and run heavy industries. He criticized the socialists' belief that the state is a better producer and distributor of goods than the private parties and cautioned against indiscriminate and needless nationalization of industries. He wrote in this regard:

"Nationalization [of industries] is worthwhile only if the Government can manage the industries

efficiently. But this is difficult. We have neither the men nor the resources even to run our administration... Let those who have the knowledge and experience manage the industries and increase the country's wealth."

If the government borrowed money from public, domestic financial institutions or foreign countries to set up or nationalize industries, it would cause further deterioration of the economy as the state's ability to earn profit on such investments reduces. If the government had to have any role in the industrial sector, it should be in the small-scale and village industries sector.

Unlike the left-wing politicians, the Sardar did not consider profit motive as intrinsically bad or evil. He was realistic enough to understand that without the scope for profit and individual gain, no industrialist would be willing to set up an industry. He felt that it was possible to earn profit with honesty and integrity. If the economic policies gave such a scope, the development of the country would be faster. However, he did not leave any opportunity to urge the industrialists to act in a spirit of trusteeship and use their profit not just for their own benefit but spare a substantial part of it for national development and welfare measures for the society. Reminding the industrialists of their responsibilities towards the nation, he remarked in one of his speeches to the businessmen:

"I...acknowledge that profit motive is a great stimulant to exertion and rules human conduct in whatever walk of life it may be, whether it is the capitalist the middle classes, the labour or the agricultu sts with whom we may have to deal. At the same me, transcending everything must be a high sens of civil consciousness and national duty. What wo ld riches avail those who have hoarded wealth, f the economic problems of the country remain unsolved and lead to chaos?" [2]

The Need for Private Property

The question of private property has been one of the most controversial social and economic ideas in all times. In modern times, the socialists have attacked private property as the main source of inequality, exploitation and poverty in societies, while the capitalists have defended it as a necessary condition for production, prosperity and economic growth. The Sardar defended the right to private property as essential for economic development and pleaded before the Constituent Assembly for giving it the status of a fundamental right though the socialist members strongly opposed this proposal. It would not be an exaggeration to say that but for the Sardar's forceful stand, right to property might not have found a place in Chapter III of the Indian Constitution. The Sardar also disapproved of the forcible land redistribution in rural areas through legislative measures. While fully sympathizing with the plight of the poor and landless farmers, he believed that the confiscation of land of the large landowners for distribution among the marginal or landless farmers was not the solution to the problem of poverty in the agricultural sector.

Criticism of Socialism

The Sardar had no liking for the dogmas and slogans of the socialists within or outside the Congress Party. He used to criticize them for their simplistic analyses of India's socioeconomic realities and for being over impressed by the Soviet experience. Poking fun at their factionalism, he once remarked:

"We are told that there are eighty-four castes among the Brahmins, but judging by their disputes and differences, I think there must be eighty-five varieties of socialists."[3]

He believed that the socialists' advocacy of redistribution of wealth was not helpful as there was not enough wealth to be redistributed in India. Instead, more emphasis should be placed on producing wealth first and then consider the modalities of its redistribution.

The Goal of Increased Production

Sardar Patel considered increasing production and growth as the most important challenges before the Indian economy. Increased production is the only means by which we can reach higher level of growth. Unless India produced more of the agricultural and industrial goods, there will be little scope of removing poverty and inequality. In a speech in February 1948 he said:

"The future of India depends on how much more we can produce in the matter of food grains, clothes, iron, cement and other things required for the common man as well as for the army. This is not only necessary to remove poverty, but also essential to strengthen the Independence which our country has secured by paying high costs, and sacrifice and also with self- confidence." [4]

Increased production would also help narrow the gap between supply and demand and contain the spiral of rising prices.

Inspiration of the Cooperative Movement

Sardar Patel was instrumental in inspiring the biggest cooperative movement in India. It was his motivation that helped set up the milk cooperative of farmers to market milk and dairy products in the Kaira district of Gujarat. This cooperative became the foundation stone of what was to become later the White Revolution in India. The availability of milk in India was highly inadequate as only about half of the total milk requirement was produced domestically though India boasted of about a quarter of the world's cattle population. In the Sardar's view, cooperative was the only way to augment milk supply and remove exploitation of farmers at the hands of the middlemen and the commercial company that purchased the milk. Upon his advice, his trusted lieutenant Morarji Desai organized such a milk cooperative named Kaira District Cooperative Milk Producers' Union in January 1946. Following the success of this effort, village-level cooperatives were set up throughout the Kaira district to collect milk from the producers and sell it to the government through district union. The cooperative movement helped break the monopoly of the foreign firm Polson over milk and dairy products in western India and sowed the seeds of what was to become one of the biggest dairy companies of the world, viz. *Amul*. Over the decades, *Amul* has changed the face of rural Gujarat and made hundreds of thousands of farmers partners in its prosperity. It has ensured that the farmers get the best price for their milk while the consumers also get quality milk products at the most reasonable prices. *Amul* has also become an exemplar for similar cooperative movements in India and abroad.

The Place of Labour

Sardar Patel underscored the significance of labour in the national economy and production process on whose ***"efficiency and hard work depends the greatness of the country."***[5] He suggested cooperation rather than conflict between the labour and the capital for accomplishing the goals of national development. Even as he favoured the right of the labour to fair wages and good working conditions, he advised them not to agitate or go on strike for petty problems but work for producing more goods with their full strength. If the labour wanted more wages, it should also be ready to produce more. Finding that strikes and labour unrest had become means of promoting political ends, he observed:

"Regarding strikes, I feel that is deplorable that they have been made so cheap. They are now props of leadership of labour and have ceased to be a legitimate means of redressing grievances of labour... The maxim should be 'produce and then distribute equitably'. Instead, they fight before even producing wealth."[6]

On another occasion, he remarked:

"If the labour will adopt the right course, they will strengthen the country and India's future will be glorious. Labour should keep the interest of millions of Indians before their sight and should not be misled by a wrong leadership. They should see what is in the best interests of the country."[7]

Hence, he favoured arbitration rather than militant trade unionism as the best method of resolving management-labour disputes.

Approach of Planning

The Indian government adopted the concept of economic planning and set up the Planning Commission with the objective of promoting balanced regional development and removing socio-economic inequality. Some commentators believe that as the Deputy Prime Minister, the Sardar was personally opposed to planning which he and others accepted largely due to Prime Minister Jawaharlal Nehru's insistence to replicate the Soviet planning model in India. However, this is not a correct conjecture in as much as even Sardar Patel had highlighted the merits of planning when it was being discussed in the meetings of the Congress Party prior to independence. However, he believed that only such economic planning that is based on the unique socio-economic conditions of India and the Gandhian approach to rural development, priority to agriculture and revitalizing of rural economy would have some merit.

While addressing a conference of the chief ministers in 1950, he said:

"Machinery will not solve the problem because millions of idle hands that have no work cannot find employment on machines. India's planning must necessarily differ from the planning of highly developed and industrialized countries. India is primarily an agricultural country and in a country as thickly populated as India is, idleness is the greatest disease. Gandhiji's planning was, therefore, of a different kind and it was difficult."[8]

With respect to the Planning Commission, the Sardar also cautioned:

"There should be a clear demarcation of its role so that it would not usurp the functions of Government and that planning should be realistic in terms of resources and capability."[9]

The Post-Independence Economic Policies

The economic policy of India in the first four decades after independence was formulated on the basis of the ideological and political principles laid down by the first Prime Minister of India Jawaharlal Nehru. Nehru was deeply impressed by the socialistic norms of centralized economic planning, nationalization of industry, commanding role of the state in economic growth, undermining of the profit motive and distrust of private enterprise. After his visit to the Soviet Union in 1927, Nehru became a starry-eyed admirer of the Soviet system and began advocating socialism as a panacea for India's poverty, inequality and unemployment. The Karachi Congress in 1931 and the Lucknow Congress in 1936 saw Nehru openly propagating the gospel of socialism, classless society and economic redistribution. This forceful advocacy caused such irritation among his colleagues in the Congress Working Committee that seven of them, including Sardar Patel, Rajendra Prasad and C. Rajagopalachari, resigned in protest against Nehru's attempts to take the Congress away from the Gandhian principles. Following the death of the Sardar and estrangement of Rajagopalachari from the Congress in the early 1950s, there was no substantial opposition to the attempts of Nehru to adopt the ***"socialistic pattern of society"*** as the goal of the Congress Party and the nation, pursue top-heavy industrialization and give the commanding role to the state in economic development from the second five-year plan onwards. Socialism in the later decades became a euphemism for the 'license-permit-quota Raj' that bred massive bureaucratic and political corruption and encouraged people to participate in a parallel economy run on black money. Such lopsided policies pursued till 1991 not only did not alleviate the problems of poverty and inequality but also aggravated them further. Instead of reducing the role of government and unfettering the economic potential of the people in the spirit of democracy, socialism in India led to the spread of the government to all areas of public activity and shrinkage of the sphere of the civil society. This made bureaucrats and politicians rich and powerful, businessmen dishonest and people dependent and deprived.

The Relevance of the Sardar's Economic Ideas Today

Sardar Patel's economic ideas reflect his deep concern to rescue India from the social and economic crisis around the time of its independence. They are contemporaneous and problem-oriented rather than theoretical in nature. Obviously, he could not have envisioned the economic conditions and processes of the contemporary times. Hence, in order to ascertain the contemporary relevance of the Sardar's views, one has to discern the broad trends and perspectives from his thinking and examine their applicability in the present context of India's economic strategy.

Due to his views which favoured private property, growth-oriented rather than redistributionist economic policies and primacy for agricultural sector, the Sardar has been given several epithets like capitalist, feudalist, rightist, conservative, a friend of the rich people and so on by the left-leaning politicians and commentators. These critics would want us to believe that but for the Sardar, Nehru could have initiated his programmes of land reforms, nationalization of industries and state-monitored economic development much earlier and faster.

However, such an assessment is unfair to the Sardar's legacy. The global experience has proven that a free economy is far more efficient in achieving the goals of growth and employment-generation than a state-regulated economy that stifles entrepreneurial spirit. The high growth rates achieved by the West European economies in comparison to the East European and Soviet economies justify the apprehensions expressed by the Sardar before and after independence about taking the Indian economy in the direction of socialism. In the age of globalization and liberalization, states are vying with each other for removing controls on economic enterprises and disinvesting their holdings in companies. This realization has dawned in India after suffering low growth rate, sluggish employment situation and continuation of poverty for forty years under the regime of command economy, Soviet-style planning and policies ostensibly aimed at 'the socialistic pattern of society'. Today, it is fashionable to talk of private enterprise, free market and limited government as desirable attributes of the state. Consensus prevails on moving along the path of liberalization and globalization for rapid growth and staying competitive in the emerging environment. Recognizing the futility of investing public funds into unviable and unprofitable public sector units, the government has set out an agenda of privatization and disinvestment of these units. However, after more than a decade of economic liberalization, India still ranks 122 in the world economic freedom index.

After Mahatma Gandhi, the Sardar was probably the biggest supporter of the interests of rural India and farmers. Agriculture contributes most to the gross domestic product, national income and exports of India. Development of the agriculture to the fullest capacity holds the key to India's economic transformation. India also has a comparative advantage over other countries in several agricultural commodities like cotton, wheat and rice. However, governments in the post-independence period have not heeded the Sardar's advice and neglected the imperative of agricultural growth.

Due to the Sardar's insistence, the first five-year plan rightly focused on the agricultural sector and developing irrigation and other rural infrastructure. However, after his departure, few hurdles remained in the path of the planners to make agriculture subservient to industry and keep agricultural production, trade in agricultural commodities and their pricing under tight government regulations. From the second five-year plan onwards, there has been a steady decline in the allocation for the agricultural sector in real terms. Rather than addressing the genuine problems of agriculturists, for political purposes, income tax exemption to agricultural income and a regime of unviable agricultural subsidies in fertilizers and debt repayment has been introduced to benefit the medium and large farmers. Such subsidies have little bearing on the destiny of the small and marginal farmers who make up the large majority of the Indian farmers.

Although the green revolution has resulted in self-sufficiency of food, the importance of generating food surplus that could be exported to other countries and made a source of extra income for the villages has not been understood. Productivity in Indian agriculture remains lower than the advanced nations. The investments in the mechanization of farming, introduction of new agricultural technologies, irrigation, research of new seeds, etc., have been insufficient. Farm subsidies and irrational controls have held back the process of liberalizing the agricultural sector and increasing the role of market forces. Budget after budget in the recent years have offered numerous sops to the industrial sector. However, the same concessions and concerns for removing controls on agriculture are missing. Such neglect of the agricultural sector can also prove a constraint for industries, as agricultural growth and industrial growth are interdependent and complementary. Modernization and development of the agriculture also have a multiplier effect on the industrial sector. There is no doubt that a lot can be gained by incorporating the Sardar's ideas on agriculture and rural India in today's economic policies.

Conclusion

Sardar Patel was a fine blend of idealism and realism who detested dogmas of political or economic kind. He was not a doctrinaire thinker but one who was most concerned about the good of the common man through policies that are practicable rather than through steps that may seem ideal but difficult to put into practice. His pragmatic approach, realism and roots in the rural Indian society would have helped a lot in shaping India's economic policies because, as one commentator has remarked about Sardar Patel:

"Our country has no dearth of theoreticians. But it is woefully deficient in the art of execution.

It does not understand that the great questions of the day are settled not by speeches and resolutions but by determined and diligent action. Ideas are important. But it is constructive work alone that can inject meaning into the veins of history and civilization." [11]

In the context of the shift in the post-independence India's economic policies, one cannot but admire the Sardar for emphasizing liberal economic and political principles in an era in India when such advocacy was considered sacrilegious by the dominant socialist voices. Had the Sardar's thoughts on production, agriculture, rural India, private enterprise, nationalization of industries and planning been heeded by India's policy makers, the path of India's development would have taken a qualitatively different trajectory.

References

1. Nani Palkhivala, *We the Nation, the Lost Decades* [New Delhi: UBS, 1994], p. 259-266.
2. Cited by Manoj Soni, "A Bibliography and Monograph on Sardar Patel" [Vallabh Vidyanagar, 2002], p. 29.
3. *For a United India: Speeches of Sardar Patel 1947-1950* [New Delhi: Publications Division, Government of India, 1982], p. 84.
4. Quoted by B. K. Murthi, *Sardar Patel: The Man and His Contemporaries* [New Delhi: Sterling, 1976], p. 90.
5. Cited by M. C. Bhatt, "Relevance of Sardar Patel's Economic Ideas Today", www.pic.nic.in
6. *For a United India: Speeches of Sardar Patel 1947-1950, op. cit.*, p. 75.
7. *For a United India: Speeches of Sardar Patel 1947-1950, op. cit.*, p. 73.
8. Cited by M. C. Bhatt, *op. cit.*
9. *For a United India: Speeches of Sardar Patel 1947-1950, op. cit.*, p. 93.
10. V. Shankar, *My Reminiscences of Sardar Patel*, Volume II [New Delhi: Macmillan, 1975], p. 107.
11. V.Y. Kantak, "The Sardar and His Manysplendoured Legacy", www.dailyexcelsior.com, 16 November, 2000.

9
Administrative Skills of Sardar Vallabhbhai Patel

S. Vincent De Paul

Introduction

India is a country having multi geographical regions. People speaking different languages and following different cultures, customs and taboos are living harmoniously in India. Thus the country, India is proud of having unity in diversity. No doubt this has been achieved due to the administrative skills of Sardar Vallabhbhai Patel. If he had not united the smaller states, India would have lost the pride of unity in diversity. The administrative skills of Sardar Vallabhbhai Patel holds stand past, present and future situations. This article tries to pay attention to the administrative skills of Sardar Vallabhbhai Patel.

Boldness

The skill of having boldness is one of the administrative skills hold by fruit of India and the Jhaverbhai and Ladbai namely Sardar Vallabhbhai Patel. He possessed this skill even in his high school times. He moved to Nadiad for high school form Petlad. There, one teacher had the habit of going to the classroom with a stick. One day the teacher gave severe punishment to one of his classmates with the stick. Sardar Vallabhbhai Patel boldly decided to make a full stop to this kind of arrogant nature of the teacher. He asked the students to vacate the classroom and made a boycott continuously for three days. On third day he succeeded and the teacher came to classroom without stick. He led 50 students even in his student hood.

During his schooling one teacher compelled the students to buy pencil and books from him. Sardar Vallabhbhai Patel opposed the business carried out by the teacher. He made the teacher to stop doing business by his boldness and leading the student team.

Even in his school age period he jumped into the local body election and made an electoral campaign for a reputed teacher who contested against a multimillionaire without having fear towards manpower and money power and looking only character power.

Perseverance

All administrators should have perseverance. Though all are aware that perseverance conquers all, many administrators do not follow it. But Sardar Vallabhbhai Patel followed it and made his followers also to follow it. During the British period, a slavery system was followed when government employees came to village for executing their work. During their village visit, the potter, barber, dhobi and scavenger had to the work for the government servants without getting any remuneration. Sardar Vallabhbhai Patel strongly condemned it and decided to stop this kind of slavery. He wrote to the government officials. They did not reply. He gave pamphlets to the workers of the village with his followers. He insisted the workers to demand remuneration for their work without loosing their fundamental rights. At last he brought change among the workers. It was his first public life victory.

Common Goal

Administrators should be away from selfishness. They should pay much more attention to the common people problems. Sardar Vallabhbhai Patel had that skill. The proceedings of *Gujarat Sabha* were held in foreign language English. People did not understand the proceedings of *Gujarat Sabha*. He under the chairmanship of Gandhi conducted the proceedings in Gujarati. The people understood the proceedings and benefited. The *Gujarat Sabha* became a forum for activity centred under the Chairmanship of Gandhi and the Secretariat of Sardar Vallabhbhai Patel.

Receiving and Respondingness

An administrator should have the skill of listening the problem and receiving it, and finally responding it sympathetically and forwarding it to the higher authorities for an appropriate action. Sardar Vallabhbhai Patel was excellent in these kinds of skills. In 1918, at Kaira district due to flood the harvest was very poor. Government exempted from land tax for those who had got harvest below 25%. In all most all the villages of the Kaira district had the harvest below 25%. But the government declared only 103 villages out of 603 villages as a harvest below 25%.

The affected villagers approached Sardar Vallabhbhai Patel. He keenly observed their problems and passed it to Gandhi. Our national *Guru* Gandhi accepted to lead the meaningful agitation but asked a commander for the force. Sardar Vallabhbhai Patel, though he got barrister degree, he gave it out and accepted to lead the force as commander with full open mindedness. From that day onwards Sardar Vallabhbhai Patel devoted his life and time for the prosperity of nation India.

On March 22nd 1918, Sardar Vallabhbhai Patel participated in the agitation under the leadership of Gandhi. The Government ordered to capture the land for that the tax had not been paid by the farmers. The government auctioned the materials and the cattle chased by the government from the farmers houses that did not pay the tax for their land. Sardar Vallabhbhai Patel maintained the will power of the farmers. Finally the agitation was made successful. Gandhi had pointed out that the Sardar Vallabhbhai Patel was the gold refined in a fire for a long time.

Decision Making

Decision Making is the most important skill necessary to lead a government or an organization. Most of our administrators are not having this kind of skill and hence we are lacking in many progress. But Sardar Vallabhbhai Patel was a mentor in this kind of skill. In 1924, Sardar Vallabhbhai Patel became the president of Municipality of Ahmedabad. To reduce the congestion in the town he introduced Kankaria Town Extension Project. He made Ahmedabad municipality as a model municipality.

On 23rd July 1927, Ahmedabad experienced a rain that could not be seen in the history. The rain stopped only on 29th July 1927. Within a week 130cm was rained. 6000 houses fallen and 50000 people became houseless. The fertile lands of Gujarat and cattle became a waste of the state. People ran pillar to pillar for minimizing the hungry. Seeing this situation, Sardar Vallabhbhai Patel made the Congress as an active organization and established many relief centres. He requested the people to donate for relief measures. People donated with humbleness.

Ultimately the government of Bombay and the Government of India gave 0.13 cores and 1 crore respectively for relief and rehabilitation work. Sardar Vallabhbhai Patel handled the situation smoothly without any hastiness.

Pinpointing the Problems

Administrators should have the skill of identifying the problems from the environments. Sardar Vallabhbhai Patel had that skill. He came to Tamilnadu by accepting the Rajaji's invitation. He observed while touring in Tamilnadu that due to Periyar's *Suyamariyathai* Movement there was a cleavage between the *Brahmins* and *Non-Brahmins* when a comparison was made in education and employment. He emphasized unity among them by pointing out that Super *Brahmin* who came from England pressed both *Brahmins* and *Non-Brahmins*. He further stated that the England people could be sent out if we were united together.

Tactfulness

Administrators must have the skill of tactfulness since they meet different kind of people having different kinds of problems. Sardar Vallabhbhai Patel had this kind of skill in him. After the Independence the affected people came from Pakistan disturbed the Muslims living in Delhi. Due to the strong actions and perseverance of Sardar Vallabhbhai Patel normal life was restored in Delhi. On 30th September Sardar Vallabhbhai Patel went to Amritsar to prevent the religious atrocities in Punjab. He requested the Punjab people to allow the Muslim refugees going to Pakistan through Amritsar safely. He remarked that religious atrocities made the people not living smoothly in East Punjab [Muslims] West Punjab [the Hindus and Sikhs]. It was always good to carry the migration peacefully and flexibly for all. In the month of October, he went to Patiala and requested Sikhs to give away the thinking of repining on Muslims and have the spirit of peace. Through his speech using tactfulness he sublimed the fire of religious atrocities.

Concern of Education

Administrators of an organization should focus on the education/training of the employees for increasing the productivity. Similarly the rulers of the state should focus on education that will increase the productivity of the nation. Sardar Vallabhbhai Patel followed this when he functioned as a ruler. Sardar Vallabhbhai Patel paid special attention to strengthen the National Education in Gujarat. In Gujarat *Vidyapeeth* there were 250 students. In schools attached to the Gujarat Vidyapeeth 37000 students were studied. It had 75000 books. In spite of all these it did not have own buildings. Sardar Vallabhbhai Patel requested the Gujarat people to donate 10 lakhs. On 2nd October, the birthday of Gandhi, the Gujarat people donated 10 lakhs.

Long Vision

Administrators should have short vision and long vision to achieve excellence in their work. But the short visions are for solving the immediate problems. But the long vision needs more inspection. It needs more skills of planning with anticipation of the pros and cons. Sardar Vallabhbhai Patel had expertise in such a skill. He led the sub committee of fundamental rights and the committees of the powers of state and the Minority. He insisted of having a middle place in the rights of fundamentalist and the rights of developed countries. As a head of the Minority committee he spoke with open mind ness to minorities and convinced them the abolition of special reservation in election. He had three visions in his mind according to N. N. Palkhivala in Sardar Vallabhbhai Patel Memorial Lecture [1992]:

Bringing India under one rule;

To sustain the united India establishing a powerful efficient pure administration; and

To make India strong in economical and resource.

He brought his visions to reality in 1948 by accessioning 554 princely states in to the Indian Union by providing copy of *'Instrument of Accession'* without perishing the kings of states. It is really a Himalayan victory in Indian History.

Iron-Handedness

Administrators should have Iron-handedness also to some extent in order to tackle very complicated problems. Sardar Vallabhbhai Patel had it. The Nizam of Hyderabad refused to made accession with India. Nizam gave 22 cores to Pakistan as loan. He declared Hyderabad as Muslim state. The steps taken by Mountbatten went useless. After 21st June 1948, Sardar Vallabhbhai Patel involved directly in handling the accession of Hyderabad. Using Indian Army Hyderabad was captured within 108 hours. Because of this Nizam 23rd November 1948 accepted the Indian Constitution.

Conclusion

A village farmer's son turned in to lawyer, freedom fighter, leader and Bismarck because of the possession of administrative skills by Sardar Vallabhbhai Patel. His activities reflect how to do administration effectively to provide services to the society for its enrichment. His administrative skills like Boldness, Perseverance, Common goal, Receiving & Responding-ness, Decision Making, Pinpointing the problems, Tactfulness, Concern on Education, Long Vision and Iron-handedness never fails and each and every administrator may follow his skills in his organization / country/ state so that he/ she may become a successful administrator.

10

Some Aspects of Sardar Patel and His Vision of Independent India

Makrand Mehta

Although Nehru was undoubtedly a great leader, nothing is more distracting and disturbing for Indian democracy than the efforts of the Congress leaders to build up and patronize the Nehruvian dynasty for a variety of reasons. Some of the recent biographies on Sardar Patel are in response or even reaction to this ongoing phenomenon.[1] The Patel theme is well justified because next to Gandhi the Sardar was the towering leader who changed the rhythm of recent Indian history by his disruptive - innovative and creative activities. It is true that Sardar Patel did not possess the Charisma of Gandhi and Nehru, yet it has been accepted even by his contemporary political adversaries like Maulana Abul Kalam Azad that he had laboured furiously to create a modern nation.[2] The Sardar was a realist and he put flesh upon Gandhi's ideas in order to create a modern, confident and unified India.

It is not my intention to repeat what has been so lucidly and persuasively said by Sardar Patel's biographers. I would, however, like to cite just one point in order to show how he had inherited his regional and local *Patidar* roots. Even the present-day *Patidars*, by and large, do not possess eloquence and fluent imageries. They are known more for their hospitality, for their initiative and drive and independent spirit. In recent years the Patels have acquired great fame for their aggressive in the entrepreneurship.[3] This is in keeping with the *Kanbi / Patidar* tradition, especially of the agriculturally fertile *Charottar* region in the Kaira district. Bishop Heber who visited Nadiad, a little town of the district in 1825 described the Patels in the following words:

"They are very inferior in dress, manners and general appearance, to the Zamindars of Hindustan. Their manner, however, though less polished, is more independent; and here, as in Central India, instead of standing with joined hands in the presence of a superior, they immediately sit down, even if they do not advance to embrace him".[4]

Sardar Patel's entire career ever since his childhood and student days is reflected in Bishop Heber's general observations quoted above. His numerous Gujarati speeches during the freedom struggle show that in spite of Gandhi's "sobering" influence, Vallabhbhai, both as a freedom fighter and builder of the congress organization, used rough *Charottari* language in order to infuse a sense of patriotism ad discipline among the leaders as well as folks.[5] His nation building activities after the attainment of freedom show that the Sardar did not give up this style. The problems, ranging from communal and territorial to those of foreign relations were too stupendous to be tackled by idealistic or altruistic considerations.

Sardar Patel was neither a fascist nor a dictator; he was no Genghis Khan with a telephone and a gun. He was a realist who saw that the nascent democracy will not survive without discipline and patriotism and he took strong measures towards these ends only. This required strong political will and the courage to face diatribes and invectives from the top-ranking Indian politicians. The Sardar had enough of these qualities. He had learnt since his early childhood how not to submit to the dikteits.[6]

II

Sardar Patel was a political fighter and organizer and not an ideologue like Gandhi and Nehru. The basic values for which he fought show that his vision of independent India is as much relevant today as it was in the yester years. He was anti-imperialist. He shared most of the basic values of India's national liberation revolution: commitment to democracy and civil liberties, secularism, independent economic development and a pro-poor orientation.

Sardar Patel has much been misunderstood and misrepresented especially with regard to his attitude towards India's communal problem. But his actions and speeches before and after independenco amply demonstrate that with all his differences with Gandhi and Nehru in this respect, he cherished secular values. At the Jaipur session of the Congress in December 1948, he said that the Congress and the Government were determined to ***'make India a truly secular state'***.[7]

In a speech at Hyderabad in August 1949 he had declared that Muslims were not foreigners and that they had equal civic, political and economic rights in a democratic set-up. Where he differed from Gandhi and Nehru was not on secular values but on the way in looking at the communal and political situation that ultimately led to the partition of India. Being a more pragmatic leader he had reasoned that it would not be too easy for Indian Muslims to shed off their historical prejudices. Hence his famous Lucknow speech of 6 January 1948:

"I am a true friend of the Muslims although I have been described as their greatest enemy. I believe in plain speaking. I do not know how to mince matters.... I ask them [Muslim] why they do not unequivocally denounce Pakistan for attacking Indian Territory with the connivance of Frontier tribesmen. I want to say a word as a friend of Muslims that it is your duty now to sail in the same boat and sink or swim together".[8]

Later on, in 1950, a few months before his death, Sardar Patel had declared:

"Ours is a secular state. We cannot fashion our policies or shape our conduct in the way Pakistan does. We must see that our secular ideals are actually realized in practice. Here every Muslim should feel that he is an Indian citizen and has equal rights as an Indian. If we cannot make him feel like this, we shall not be worthy of our heritage and of our country".[9]

Sardar Patel had his own way of assessing the communal situation during the most troublesome years. His vision of independent secular India was tempered by practical wisdom and it provides a historical hindsight to the nation in its attempts to safeguard its multilingual, multicultural and multiethnic heritage.

The same objective led Patel to work for the nationalization of the Indian army. As early as in 1928 when Patel emerged as a national hero, Mahadev Desai wrote his brief biography in which he quoted the Sardar in the following words: ***"There is nothing better in my life more than that I like a good fight"***. The leader of the Bardoli *Satyagraha* had mobilized the masses against the atrocities of an alien rule before and during the *Satyagraha*. The same spirit led the Sardar to mobilize the masses against the rulers of the princely states that refused to merge with the Indian Union. At the same time he enthused the army on January 2, 1998 in the following words:

"Freedom has brought responsibilities unfortunately mixed with trouble in its wake. The army is being nationalized. You fought gallantly in the past and proved yourself first class fighters. Now you have to fight for your own country under your own government. Let yours be the privilege to do this job and enhance and guard the reputation of Free India". [10]

The way in which Sardar Patel brought about the integration of princely states with the union government shows his foresightedness and statesmanship. Junagarh and Hyderabad provide the classic examples of his statesmanship and his skills in mobilizing the masses against the princes who refused to oblige. Without the popular support the bloodless revolution would not have been attained. It was indeed a miracle, observes P.N. Chopra, that the Sardar was able to achieve the merger of about 562 princely states comprising one-third of the total area of India into the Indian Union within a short span of less than two years.[11] To bring home the point that the Sardar was a man of great vision, Chopra has quoted Sardar Patel's own speech which he had delivered before the constituent Assembly on 12 October 1949:

"The great ideal of geographical, political and economic unification of India, an ideal which for centuries remained a distant dream and which appeared as remote and as difficult of attainment even after the advent of Indian independence was consummated by the policy of integration." [12]

If the Sardar was a master craftsman in integrating and consolidating India, he was equally a man of vision to see the possible aggressions from India's neighbours, particularly China and Pakistan. In his foresighted vision, he had foreseen the Chinese threat to our northern border after the Chinese aggressive policies towards Tibet and Nepal. His oft-quoted letter to Prime Minister, Jawaharlal Nehru dated 7-11-1950 is a case in point. In that letter he had warned Nehru that the Communist Government of China were trying to delude India by professing the ideals of 'peaceful co-existence' and that the country could not afford to be complacent or vacillating.

Nehru however had a flair for leftist ideas and he did not listen to the Home Minister's advice. He had been keener to test and apply his ideals of *Panchsheel* in the realm of international politics. The Chinese aggression on India in 1962 thus, followed in the wake of the slogan ***Hindi-Chini Bhai- Bhai***, and was politically its sequel. The lonesome Prime Minister in his pensive mood is said to have murmured, ***"I am finished. The Nation is humiliated."***

The political situation in India as well as international politics has undergone a great change since 1950. But the Sardar's realistic vision provides a lot of warnings and lessons to India's ruling elite. Just look at the most recent events. The Tibetan refugee is dead after immolating himself on 27 April, 1998 in protest against the five-day visit of General F.U. Quanyou, Chief of China's People's Liberation Army to establish ***"personal rapport at the political and military levels"***, and to ***"strengthen bilateral ties"*** with India for ***"global peace and regional stability"***.

It is well-known that among the other countries, China has been providing its technological assistance to Pakistan's nuclear and missile programme. In spite of China's denial, there is a widespread belief that without China's direct assistance, Pakistan could not have succeeded in testing its ICBM "Ghauri". This was followed on 26 April, 1998 by an optimistic statement of Abdul

Kalam, Defence Adviser to Prime Minister Atal Behari Vajpayee, that since ***"India has the capacity and the preparedness to manufacture all sorts of nuclear weapons"*** we should not worry about the Ghauri threat!

We are too close to the fast changing events to make clear judgments. But one thing is certain. China and the other world powers like the United States do not have a high regard for India's capacity to defend her against foreign aggressions. It is also certain that we have not overcome the China syndrome. Unlike India, China has always taken a *pragmatic* view of the international situation. This seems to be equally true of Pakistan. Both these countries believe that they are equipped with superior armaments. And this has enhanced the spirit of their common people also.

How would Sardar Patel have viewed this situation? And how would he have responded? It is impossible to give a clear-cut answer. But one may like to guess that he would have taken an *equally pragmatic* view of the global situation and bi-lateral talks. The Sardar would also have almost certainly galvanized the army and other defence wings with the latest equipments. This is because he had visualized the army as a vibrant and dynamic instrument of India's glory in international world. He had also visualized India as a strong, disciplined and united democratic nation.

References

1. For instance Rajmohan Gandhi, *Patel: A Life* [Ahmedabad, 1990]; P.N. Chopra. *The Sardar of India: Biography of Vallabhbhai Patel* [New Delhi, 1995]; Gunvant Shah, *The Peerless Sardar* [Ahmedabad, 1984]; R.K. Murthi, *Sardar Patel The Man and His Contemporaries* [New Delhi, 1976].
2. For details see Abul Kalam Azad, *India Wins Freedom* [Calcutta, 1959].
3. Dwijendra Tripathi and Makrand Mehta, *Business Houses in Western Indian A Study in Entrepreneurial Response 1850-1956* [New Delhi, 1990].

4. Quoted in David Hardiman, *Peasant Nationalists of Gujarat Kaira District 1917-1934* [Bombay, 1981], p. 36.

5. P.N. Chopra [Ed.], *The Collected works of Sardar Vallabhbhai Patel*, 4 Vols. [Delhi, 1990-93]; G.M. Nandurkar [Ed.], *Sardar's Letters Mostly Unknown*, 5 Vols. [Ahmedabad, 1974-78]. The Five Volumes containing Sardar Patel's letters in the Gujarati language are very important. They are edited by Manibehn Patel and Nandurkar and published by the Navajivan Press, Ahmedabad as a part of the Sardar Patel's centenary celebrations.

   The Sardar did not consider the Mahatma as his 'boss'. He loved him. But although he had great reverence for Mahatma Gandhi, he was not a blind follower. For example, while addressing a conference in Kathiawad in 1929 he declared.

   "I am accustomed to speak bluntly. I must ask you to learn to distinguish between politeness and flattery. Many call me a blind devotee of Gandhiji, but that is not the case. I claim to have average intelligence and understanding. I have seen something of this world, so it is not likely that I would follow this half, naked person without any understanding. I was a member of a profession in which I could perhaps have become rich by misleading many, but I gave up that profession, for I learnt from this man that was the way in which I could do well to the peasants". Quoted in Susana Haredia, *A Patriot for Me: A Biographical Study of Sardar Patel*, [Bombay, 1972], pp. 64-65.

6. Bipan Chandra, *Essay on Indian Nationalism* [New Delhi, 1993], p. 175.

7. Murthi, *op.cit.,* p. 53.

8. Bipan Chandra, *op.cit.,* p. 176.

9. Quoted in P.D. Saggi [Ed], *A Nation's Homage Life and Work of Sardar Vallabhbhai Patel* [Bombay, 1954], pp. 47048.

10. Chopra, The Sardar of India, *op.cit.,* p. 96.

11. *Ibid.* p. 97.

11

Sardar Patel and Indian Muslims

Mehboob Desai

On the 4th January 1932, Sardar Patel was arrested along with Gandhiji for taking part in Civil Disobedience Movement. Both were taken to *Yeravada* jail, where Sardar stayed with Gandhiji for 16 months. During this period they used to discuss often the Hindu - Muslim problems. These discussions gave a true shape to Sardar's approach towards Muslims. As Sardar respected Gandhiji's views, Gandhiji played conspicuous role in moulding and changing Sardar's attitude towards Muslims during those days. For example, on a morning of 30.3.1932 an issue of a Muslim leader having come under discussion, Sardar Patel abruptly said:

"When a critical situation emerges, this gentleman too resorts to narrow and communal attitude and demands separate fund and appeal for the Muslims."

In reply Gandhiji said:

"He cannot be blamed for the reason. What favours do we render to the Muslims! We deal with

them as if they were untouchable. Therefore if Amtus Salam has to be sent to Deolali, can we suggest keeping her there? As a matter of fact the Hindus should advance forward. If the Hindus understand the heart of the matter, and the wall of discrimination, which has been raised, is removed, it can reduce the bitterness considerably."

Vallabhbhai argues:

"But the Muslims differ in customs they are non-vegetarian where as we believe in vegetarianism, it is impossible to stay with them in a single home."

Bapu counters:

"No, No, Hindus are no where Vegetarian except in Gujarat. Every Hindu eats meat in Punjab, Sindh, and Uttar Pradesh."[1]

On the 6th June 1932, Sardar Patel with a dismal note asked Gandhiji at Yeravada Jail:

"Is there any Muslim who pays attention to what you say?"

In reply Gandhiji said:

"Doesn't matter, it does not make any difference, but let us hope that they too open their eyes. The very base of the Satyagraha is that we should trust human nature which means at least one Muslim will certainly come out to say, 'We cannot bear if this much takes place'"[2]

On the 8th April 1933 Sardar Patel referring to Indian Muslims said to Gandhiji:

"The Muslims are tongue-tied. They do not speak a word and they are fairly co-operating the Government"

Bapu's reply was:

"The Hindu-Muslim unity is never to realize till the Muslims do not see their own welfare in the welfare of the country."[3]

Such dialogue only which had taken place between Sardar and Gandhiji at the *Yeravada* Jail had made a noticeable contribution in changing Sardar's attitude towards the Muslims and giving it a constructive mould, the effect of which is discernible in Sardar's later attitude towards the Muslims of India.

After his release from the Jail, Sardar Patel was appointed as the President of the Congress Parliamentary Board to select the candidates for the elections of State Legislative Assemblies. Those elections were being held in accordance with the 1935 State Assembly Law. Due to the leadership of Sardar Patel, the Congress ministries were formed in five states out of the eleven. During this period only Mohammad Ali Jinnah was becoming active in the political arena of the Muslim League and because of his efforts the Muslims League candidates in Bombay and U.P. had put up good performance, Talks started for the construction of united of Governments of the Congress and the Muslim League in the several states. Jawaharlal Nehru and Maulana Azad represented the Congress albeit this debate ended in failure. Several historians consider Nehru's unrealistic policy responsible for this failure. Nehru had, during the debate put a condition that at first the Muslim League should merge with the Congress, then and then only the construction of the united Govt. be considered. Sardar Patel was kept quite aloof from this debate, but when he came to know about this type of attitude of Nehru, he had said:

"If the chief leader of the Muslim League Khaliquzzaman were consulted, certain compromise would have been taken place."

Majority of the historians agree with this opinion and say that this agreement could have certainly avoided partition Gandhiji's Secretary Shri Pyarelal Writes:

"This was the mistake of a prime order so far as policy is concerned."

The news writer of the "**The Times**" of London of Delhi, Mr. Louis Horren has also written:

"After several months of partition Mr. Jinnah had told me that Nehru was responsible for partition. If the Muslim League were included in the Congress Government of 1937 in U.P., Pakistan would not have been born."[4]

The British officer Penderal Moon active in ICS before and after the Independence had also shared the opinion and said that:

"The Prime cause of the Creation of Pakistan was Congress's failure to cooperate with the league in 1937."

Franh Morays, the British historian also putting the same argument, ***"Pakistan might never have come into being' had 'Congress handled the League more tactfully after the [1937] election".***[5]

The historical events are analyzed under these types of 'IFS' and 'THEN', but the essence of all such arguments is that Sardar was kept aloof from all such discussions. If Sardar who was protagonist in the merger of Princely States in Indian Union, if he were the participant of this debate, the history of India after Independence would have been certainly different from what it is.

After this event, the communal and separatist tendency of League leader Mohammad Ali Jinnah intensified; which can be seen in his communal speeches. Sardar Patel was much perturbed with Mr. Jinnah's speeches vomiting communal poison and the Muslim community was consciously led away by a Muslim leader whose aim was to shatter and bring to pieces the Hindu - Muslim unity. Sardar found it impossible to understand why Maulana Azad, who had digested the Islam deeply, hesitated to expose Jinnah's hollowness. Mohammad Ali Jinnah hardly possessed the principles of a true

Muslim. He never remained strictly faithful to the Islamic Principles like following the five times Namaz everyday and abstinence from alcohol. The question as to why the staunch Muslims still followed Jinnah puzzled Sardar. However, Sardar Patel expressed in public his internal desire for communal harmony against Jinnah's speeches vomiting communal poison. In the year 1936, in U.P., as a president of the farmer's gathering he had said:

"The kisan Community cannot have such differences as Hindu & Muslim or of one caste or the other, a cultivator who produces corn with his hard labour, a small land owner, a farmer, or a labourer helping the farmer in cultivation, let them belong to any faith or caste, are all farmers only. All are sailing in the same boat; all will sink in or swim out together. Nature never sees such differences of religion or caste. Nature is impartial when it strikes on them in the form of a natural calamity or showers favours on them. The monetary suffering of all the farmers is equal. Our sufferings will end only then when we all remain faithful to our faith and sect, setting aside differences, bringing end to communal infightings joins together in the mission of economic, social and political uplift."[8]

Jinnah's Communal Policy was naturally supported by the British Govt. as a result of which his efforts to disturb communal harmony met some success, which led him to rumblings with granted enthusiasm and greater malice - such as:

"Congress wishes to establish The Hindu Raj" while refusing this statement of Jinnah, Sardar Patel had said in the 11th session of the Legislative Assembly at Rajpipla as the President on the 25th December 1937:

"The nation's legislative assembly is a formidable organization which seeks independence not for 25 crores of its people but it aspires for the same goal

for 35 crores that includes Hindus, Muslims, Parsees, Christian and all others taken together." [7]

This policy of Sardar had received positive response from the people in his activities of public concern. The Congress Session of February 1938 was conducted entirely under his supervision. He had selected Haripura Village on the bank of the river Tapi in the Bardoli *Taluka* for the Congress session. At that time not only the Hindus but the Muslim farmers also had spared their 500 acres of land of the village for this session, with least hesitation.

Sardar had obtained as much trust and affinity with the Muslim leaders as he had from and with the Hindus by the end of 1938, Subhas Chandra Bose decided that he wished to continue as a Congress President for the second year also. Sardar Patel did not like this declaration of Subhas Babu. Many reasons were of course responsible for this. Gandhiji also had thought of the name of Maulana Azad for it. And Sardar Patel had supported this view of Gandhiji.

Maulana Azad, however, expressed his unwillingness to accept the Presidentship of the Congress but agreed to accept it after the long discussion with Gandhiji and Sardar at Bardoli on January 1939. Referring to this Sardar Patel wrote to Rajendra Babu.

"We have been able to persuade Maulana to accept the responsibility.... After hesitation for a long time he has given his assent to it."

After Maulana Azad's consent having been given, Vallabhbhai Patel also took back his candidature formally. But Maulana Azad after returning to Bombay from Bardoli changed his early decision and approached Gandhiji to make himself free from his early consent of acceptance of the Presidentship. Maulana Azad, who was himself the resident of Calcutta, perhaps felt that it might he unfair and may be unpleasant to indulge in rivalry with another Bengali. However, Subhas Babu had been elected with 1580 against 1375 as a President on the 29th of January 1939.[8]

But the fact that the manner in which Vallabhbhai had accepted Gandhiji's opinion of suggesting the name of Maulana Azad in place of the name of Subhas Babu, for the Presidentship of the Congress, itself exhibits Sardar's mind as far more inclined towards Communal Harmony as being communal.

References

1. Mahadevbhai's Diary, Volume-1, p. 65.
2. Parikh Narhari, Sardar Vallabhbhai Part-II, p. 109.
3. Mahadevbhai's Diary, Vol.-3, p. 222.
4. Zakaria, Rafiq, Sardar Patel and Indian Muslims, p. 37.
5. Gandhi, Rajmohan, Patel A Life, p. 262.
6. Parikh, Narhari and Shah, Uttamchand [Editors] Speeches of Sardar Vallabhbhai p. 33.
7. Parikh & Shah, Speeches of Sardar Patel, p. 416.
8. Gandhi, Rajmohan, Patel A Life, p. 279.

12

Sardar Patel and Integration of The Baroda State in The Indian Union

Rizwan Kadri

Most of the works on the integration of Indian princely states with the Union Government State that after the *Maharaja* of Jodhpur, although reluctantly, acceded to India, States like Patiala, Gwalior, Baroda and Bikaner, followed the suit. But the problem was not simple. Sardar Patel and his lieutenant like V.P. Menon had to come in confrontation with *Maharaja* Pratapsinh, and his ill-advisers. In fact they had to infuse a new spirit in the Baroda *Praja Mandal* in its fight against the *Maharaja*. This paper aims in describing and analyzing how Sardar Patel achieved his mission.

Baroda was fortunate in having a liberal and progressive ruler like *Maharaja* Sayajirao Gaekwad [1861-1939]. He had started an experiment of free and compulsory education in his State as early as 1906. In 1916 he initiated another experiment which resulted in the setting up of the *Praja Mandal*. It held its first convention in 1926 and since then it provided a training ground to the politically and socially oriented citizens of the State for demanding civic and political rights.

After Sayajirao's death in 1939, however, his grandson, Pratapsinh who ascended the throne, ignored the wishes of his people to get liberal treatment. The time was fast changing. The country as a whole was fighting its last battles against an alien rule for final independence. The *Praja Mandal* led by dedicated nationalists like Chootabhai Sutaria, Darbar Gopaldas and C.P. Shah was in constant touch with Sardar Patel in its attempts to get fair treatment from the State. In fact Sardar had earlier presided over the *Praja Mandal* convention held in Mehsana in North Gujarat in April 1940. This had enthused the Baroda leaders to propagate the 'rights of the citizens' as well as to spread constructive activities in the remotest rural areas of the Baroda State.

But Pratapsinh refused to see the writings on the wall. As the demand for self government increased, the *Maharaja* started squandering money from the State treasury. He had already married Shantadevi in 1929. She had borne him eight children. But in 1944 Pratapsinh married Sitadevi, who had a son by her first husband. She dissolved marriage by embarrassing Islam and eventually got married with Pratapsinh. This episode created a great uproar both in the Palace and outside it. Thereafter Pratapsinh raised his privy purse from Rs. 23 *lakhs* to Rs. 50 *lakhs* a year. He started selling ancestral jewellery worth crores of rupees.

Sardar Patel got concerned at this stage. He sent Menon to Baroda in January 1948 to negotiate with the *Maharaja*. But Pratapsinh put impossible conditions before he would accede to the Indian Union. They were as follows:

1. The Indian Dominion shall pass on to Baroda jurisdiction of all the six agencies, viz., Mahikantha, Rewakantha, Sabarkantha and Palanpur etc.
2. The ruler of Baroda should be declared the King of Gujarat and Kathiawad, so as to have sovereign powers.
3. The State of Baroda undertakes to remain a faithful ally of the Indian Dominion and shall carry out its obligations so far as the three dominion subjects, viz., Defence, External Affairs and Communications are concerned.

Sardar Patel now became tough with the *Maharaja*. He encouraged the *Praja Mandal* to launch a series of peaceful agitations against the State. As a result, Pratapsinh agreed to set up an interior popular ministry responsible to legislature. Dr. Jivraj Mehta was to be the Dewan of Baroda.

The *Maharaja*, however, postponed his 'decision'. Vallabhbhai, exercising his authority as the Home Minister, wrote him back:

"I should like to remind you that when we were in difficulties about Junagarh our approach to you met with a reply which shocked me beyond words. You bargained about your own position at a time when India was in difficulties... You have taken pride in being a popular ruler and more constitutional than any in India. But, again under misguided advice, Your Highness, behind the back of Menon and Darbar Gopaldas, with whom you had come to a definite agreement, both regarding Dr. Jivraj Mehta and regarding the text of announcement, have made changes which are both changes of substance and on the face of it in the direction of whittling down what was previously granted. Moreover, some other States gave better

reforms some months ago whereas in Baroda it was only the pressure of public opinion that made Your Highness act after so much delay."

Pratapsinh had no other alternative after receiving this stern letter. In April, 1948 he approved Mehta as the head of the interim ministry. A few days after doing so the *Maharaja* left for Europe in May 1948 without approving the names of other ministers. Jıvraj Mehta discovered that the *Maharaja*, through his secret agents, was making huge withdrawals of money.

Dr. Jivraj now consulted Sardar Patel. The Home Minister gave secret advice to Mehta to work out a plan for deposing the unruly prince. While the *Maharaja* was still in Europe, the Legislative Body, although it had no legal status to pass such a motion against the ruler, declared that Pratapsinh had forfeited the confidence of the people and that he should abdicated in favour of his son, Fatehsinh Gaekwad.

This, along with popular agitations, had a salutary effect. The *Maharaja* immediately left Europe and ran down to Delhi. He told the Sardar that would soon give complete responsible Government. But this did not happen. Eventually the Bombay Government took over the administration of the Baroda State on 1 May 1949.

The fact that the ruler of Baroda proved troublesome even after the death of Sardar Patel on 15 December 1950 shows that even the milder States like Gwalior and Baroda had created problems. Pratapsinh, even after the merger of the Baroda State used to visit Baroda territories and created a feeling of disaffection among the people against the Indian Government by his fiery speeches. The Indian Government now took a hard decision and in April 1951 deposed him as the ruler of the Baroda State.

The case of Baroda shows the role which the *Praja Mandal* and later on the popular legislature and State Ministry played in creating public opinion against the misdeeds of the *Maharaja*. At the initial stage, as the correspondence between Sardar Patel and *Maharaja* Pratapsinh show, the Sardar was polite and lenient towards Pratapsinh. He relied more on appeals; he appealed to him citing the example of his illustrious grandfather. He also appealed in the name of patriotism. It was only after the Sardar got convinced about the *Maharaja*'s tactful recalcitrance that he began to be stern with him. The following extract of the de-recognition order shows that Baroda was not peaceful as it is generally made out to be. The Order stated that the Government of India had for some time in past been considering with grave concern the activities of Pratapsingh. The activities in which he had been indulging since his installation on the *Gaddi* in 1939 were well-known, especially to the people of Baroda. His dissipation of *Crores* of rupees of public funds had also been the subject of discussion in the *Dhara Sabha* of Baroda. His activities after coming into force of the Constitution of India have been particularly objectionable. He challenged the Constitution of India and contended that the merger of Baroda with Bombay was brought about without his concurrence and was not warranted by the terms of his agreement with the Government of India. The Government of India pointed out to him that, in challenging the validity of the merger and the Indian Constitution, he had indulged in an act of disloyalty to the country.

The Government served the order to Pratapsinh on 12 April 1951. It was in the name of the President of India who had been vested this power under Article 366[22] of the Constitution.

The case of Baroda shows Sardar Patel was quite polite with the *Maharaja* in the beginning and that he had taken great care in adopting persuasive methods. It was only at a later period that the Sardar encouraged the popular leaders of Baroda to start agitations against the ruler.

Sardar Patel was indeed the architect of united and modern India. He has been rightly hailed as the Bismarck of Independent India who saved the infant nation from the disruptive activities of the princely states. Some critics have charged that the Sardar went too far on the question of Privy Purses and private property of the princes like Pratapsinhrao of Baroda. But the Sardar justified his stand by moving Article 291 of the Constitution which said that we have to pay this price for this "Bloodless Revolution". This was not a small achievement.

References

Gujarati Sources

1. Narhari Parikh, *Sardar Vallabhbhai*, 2 Vols. [Ahmedabad, 1950].
2. Manibehn Patel [Ed], *Sardarna Patro*, 5 Vols. [Ahmedabad, 1975-1978]
3. Chunilal P. Shah, *Vadodara Rajya Prajamandal non Itihas* [Baroda, 1933]
4. Pankaj Desai, *Vadodara Rajya Prajamandal* [Ahmedabad, 1988]

English Sources

1. V.P. Menon, *The Story of the Integration of the Indian States, Reprint* [Bombay, 1969]
2. G.M. Nandurkar [Ed], *This was Sardar The Sardar Commemorative Volume.* [Ahmedabad, 1974]
3. P.N. Chopra, *Towards Freedom, 1937-47, Vol. 1 Experiments with Provincial Autonomy* [New Delhi, 1985]
4. The Sardar Patel of India: *Biography of Vallabhbhai Patel* [New Delhi, 1995].
5. R.K. Murthi, *Sardar Patel The Man and His Contemporaries* [New Delhi, 1976]
6. Gazetteer of India, Gujarat State, Vadodara District [Ahmedabad, 1980]

13

Sardar Patel: A Great Human Being and Statesman

Johannes Dragsbaek Schmidt

Vallabhbhai Patel, affectionately called as the 'SARDAR' by his countrymen, was one of the great statesmen of twentieth century. He will always be remembered as a dedicated devoted and fearless freedom fighter ready to pay any price for seeking his country free from shackles of the foreign rule.

India becomes free in 1947. After freedom it was all the more necessary to preserve the freedom in a country like India having many languages with a chequered history. Moreover, India, at that time, was divided in 600 parts** in which different rulers used to govern the people in their own way. They had a good following also. But Sardar Patel, as a great human being and statesman, was suited in convincing the monarchs of princely states about the necessity of coming together and work for maintaining the freedom of country achieved with great sacrifices. In this task the firmness of the great Sardar Patel along with the sagacity of no mean order worked wonders and brought them together.

** They were known as "*Riyasats*" [princely states].

History will have admitted that Sardar Patel's firm action against the Nizam of Hyderabad[1] was helpful in annexing the State to the Union of India as well as the victory over the State of Junagarh can hardly be exaggerated.

All the qualities of a good administrator, bold and firm in principle and ready to make necessary compromises, were evinced and no wonder that his mark as the Maker of United India can never be forgotten.

Sardar Patel's love for humanity, perfection and idealism; his love for his countrymen as well as for each and everyone on the earth could be judged well from the following words of Mahatma Gandhi who stayed with him in the *Yeravada* Central Prison for more than 16 months during 1932-33:

"One of the greatest joys of my life was that I had an opportunity of staying in prison with the Sardar. I knew of his invincible courage and of his burning love for our county, but never before had I the good fortune of spending so much time with him as I was able to do during these sixteen months. His affection and love overwhelmed me and reminded me of my dear mother. I would never have imagined that he possessed such qualities of maternal affection. If I was in the slightest degree indisposed, he would be immediately by my side, and would pay personal attention to the smallest of my needs."

Reference

1. Comprising three linguistic areas and predominantly Hindu in the composition of its population the Hyderabad State provided a peculiar problem for Sardar Vallabhbhai Patel. Its ruler-the Nizam had refused to join the Union of India. He was one of those rulers [of princely states] who desired to stay independent. Like Maharaja Hari Singh-the ruler of the State of Jammu and Kashmir, the Nizam too had

visions of being the head of an independent territory enjoying the status of a dominion like India or Pakistan. Ignoring advice of Lord Mountbatten and other British Officials, he did not agree to merge the State with the Union. When no alternative course remained open to the Government of India and the situation in the State of Hyderabad continued to deteriorate, Sardar Vallabhbhai Patel, on March 13, 1948, sent Indian troops to the State. On September 17, 1948 the Nizam surrendered and agreed to merge the State with India.

14

From Spark to Flame: Patel, Gandhi and The Gujarat Congress

Shirin Mehta

The history should be constantly re-written as there is a felt need to re-evaluate Sardar's contribution to the making of modern India. In order to provide some more clues to the understanding of his complex personality and to comprehend his regional roots the micro level paper is prepared. Since Vallabhbhai presents the case of strong territorial identity the paper aims to undertake regional survey to reflect the significant and meaningful dimensions of the ideals of his life and work of great importance which had shaped the country's history. The purpose of the paper is to highlight the regional canvass of Vallabhbhai's activities that generally get subsumed a little too readily under the rubric of his much-celebrated splendorous achievements at national level. The regional approach though considered as a heuristic device, getting juxtaposed against over arching urge for national integration the spatial and componential look deepens our insight. In fact Patel's intense sense of patriotism, vision of rural and national India remained a subjective phenomena produced by varying combinations of objective factors.

Vallabhbhai Patel reputed as the main architect of the Indian administration model. He was also considered archetypal organizer and perfect party leader. He was honoured as President of All India National Congress at Karachi in 1931. During the same year he served the Congress Party as a President of its Working Committee. He was also appointed as a Chairman of the Congress Parliamentary Board from 1936 to 1942. During his tenure he made the Congress a viable finest political organization in the country to run the democratic activities. He rose to the position of Deputy Prime Minister and Home Minister after independence.

He reached to the country's highest position by putting hard efforts during his preliminary years for the political development of Gujarat the place of his birth. His political formative phase from 1918-34 was spent mainly among peasants of Gujarat. He was the son of sturdy *Kisan* from Kaira district in Central Gujarat. He belonged to the Caste Patidar. The Patidars were most numerous and dominant agrarian community in Gujarat. They were known for their rural raggedness, hard work, indomitable nature and collective consciousness.

Hence my study mainly concentrates on his activities as an organizer and mass Mobilizer in Gujarat. The paper points out the dynamics and inner recesses of Patel as a Sagacious Party leader who mobilized masses through vertical and horizontal mobilization through national leaders and micro institutions like caste and community councils, village *panchayats* respectively. I have drawn heavily from my earlier fieldwork and survey I made for my Ph. D. on Bardoli *Satyagraha* [1928] in Surat district in South Gujarat. I have depended on interviews of various grass-root workers of Central and South Gujarat the heartland of Patel's activities. The study is also based on contemporary records like diaries, letters and other source material.

Patel's initial years and his relationship with Gandhi are discussed just to provide clue to his evaluation as a leader of Gujarat.

Patel's Initial Years in Politics, Politics as a Back Drop

Vallabhbhai preferred to settle down in Ahmedabad to Karamsad or Borsad his native villages in Kaira district of Central Gujarat in 1913, Ahmedabad was the big business centre, well-developed industrial town and forerunner of social reform activities in Gujarat. Ahmedabad was virtually the economic capital of Gujarat besides political one. The capitalists the men of letters became his close associates and friends. They invited him to be the councillor of the Ahmedabad Municipality in 1919. As a Chairman of the Sanitary Committee [1919-22] and later on as a President of the Municipality [1924-27] he tried to develop Ahmedabad as a model town in the country. As a man of self-respect and strong determination he was bound to enter into conflicts with the arrogance and high-handed policy of the British bureaucrats - Commissioners and Collectors. They headed the Local Self Government. Vallabhbhai made the Local Self Government a training ground for youths to win independence. Ahmedabad experience proved the most rewarding in his career.[1]

Reflection on the Dynamics of Gandhi-Patel Relationship

The emergence of Gandhi in 1915 on the political scene of Gujarat resulted into complete break through like Vallabhbhai he also preferred to make Ahmedabad the nerve centre of his activities to Porbander in

Saurashtra region the place of his birth. He came with remarkable achievement of experimenting successfully the non-violent *Satyagraha* technique as a redress of grievances in South Africa [1908-14] Gandhi initially preferred to practice the method of passive resistance in matters of local issues like the problems of peasants of Bihar.[2]

Vallabhbhai directly came into contact with Gandhi only in November, 1917. Their relationship has always been misunderstood and misrepresented. No biographer of Vallabhbhai reviewed correctly the inner recesses of their relationship except Rajmohan Gandhi to a certain extent. Vallabhbhai has been wrongly referred as ***'blind followers'***, ***'ardent disciple'*** or ***'disciplined adherent'*** of Gandhi as if he lacked his own autonomy and subjectivity.[3]

In fact Gandhi badly needed Vallabhbhai and Vallabhbhai was attracted to Gandhi on three counts:

- Vallabhbhai himself a man of practical application appreciated the action oriented and clear goal directedness in Gandhi;
- Both shared anti-imperialist stance; and
- He was enamoured of Gandhi's interest into peasants' and workers' problems - the lower segments of the society, he attributed great significance to Gandhi's mass-leader dialectics.

Gandhi attached lot of significance to masses as an important variable to uproot exploitative alien rule from India. By masses he meant peasantry. The 76 to 85 per cent of the people in India were dependent on agriculture for their livelihood. The role of a leader is to direct and to respond to the spontaneity and consciousness of the people.

Vallabhbhai was the son of the soil. His father had 10 *acres* of land in Karamsad a village in Charottar area known for its finest fertility. But the land was too meagre to provide minimum bare subsistence. He had experienced since childhood the hard realities. He had actually internalized the peasant's problems in *ryotwari* land tenure of Gujarat.[4]

It was the task of Vallabhbhai to broaden the social base of the institutions that he required to head by associating workers and peasants.

Vallabhbhai As An Organizer And Leader Of Gujarat Politics [1919-1946]

The bourgeois elites of Gujarat crystallized into various micro-institutions like Gujarat Vernacular Society [Ahmedabad, 1848], *Praja Hitvardhak Sabha* [Surat, 1882], *Gujarat Sabha* [Ahmedabad, 1884], Home Rule Leagues [in Cities of Gujarat, 1916-20], City Municipalities [1848; 1885]. These institutions were semi-political running socio-reform activities. The elite gentry were moderate in their political inclination. But the over bearing 'business culture' of Gujarat turned them the critic of government economic policy. In the beginning of the 20th Century there began to emerge the large class of small landholder proprietors as discontented element against the exploitative agrarian policy and draconian land laws of the colonial government. These classes liked collaborative efforts. They were ***'class in itself' conscious of economic interest but politically ignorant of their collective interest i.e. not 'class for itself'.***[5]

Both Gandhi and Vallabhbhai tried to revitalize the old institution like *Gujarat Sabha* when Gandhi was made its President in 1917 and Vallabhbhai was selected its Secretary. They transformed it from elite to peoples' institution and broadened its social base. *Gujarat Sabha* was made unit to carry constructive programme to serve the people Gandhi appointed an executive committee to run the action based programme through out the year. Its members were asked to organize march to Nilgiris to demand release of Mrs. Annie Besant who was arrested there for her Home Rule activities. The plan did not materialize. Vallabhbhai moved throughout Gujarat to collect signature for the memorandum demanding *Swaraj* to be presented to Edusin Montague the Secretary for India on his visit. Some 8000 signatures were collected. Under the auspices of *Sabha* the Gujarat Political Conference was convened at Godhra in the tribal Bhill area. It was decided to carry its working in local language. The innovation attracted large crowds to take interest in the deliberations. *Sabha* also launched movement against invidious practice of forced labour. Vallabhbhai forged legal battle against *Veth* and forced commission to remove it. *Sabha* had undertake awareness programme and distributed leaflets making people conscious against forced labour.[6]

Sabha was required to play a major role in 1918. Due to excessive rain in the Kaira district the crops was washed away. Even then the Government ordered to collect land revenue. The peasants resented. They took initiative and approached *Sabha* members to lead their movement Gandhi led the Kaira Peasant *Satyagraha* in 1918. It lasted hardly for few months. The absentee landholders together with the peasant women under the fear of Japti operation paid land revenue. Kaira Peasant *Satyagraha* was a failure. It could not create homogeneous cohesive structure. The women and children of Vanthli village of Matar *Taluka* beat the *Japti* officer. Also the landless labourers, tenants and subtenants like *Baraiyas* and *Patanwadias* attacked the *Patidar* and *Anavil* landholders, Gandhi could not keep the movement non-violent and within circumscribed character.[7]

After the failure of Kaira Peasant Movement, Gandhi and Vallabhbhai realized the inherent weakness of

Gujarat Sabha. It had fragile structure. It lacked organizational networking. Vallabhbhai also found Indian National Congress in Gujarat in a State of disarray.

Formation of Gujarat Provincial Congress Committee–1921

Gandhi restructured Indian National Congress in Gujarat on a British model with hierarchy of provincial, district, *Taluka* and village Congress Committees in 1921. Vallabhbhai was made its President, the position he enjoyed up to 1946, still he relinquished. Vallabhbhai's appointment was a natural corollary of the sequence. Indulal Yagnik a Nagar *Brahmin* from Nadiad, a leading journalist and enthusiastic Home Rule Leaguer was asked to be its Secretary. Gujarat Vidyapeeth a national University founded in Ahmedabad in 1920 was G.P.C.C.'s venue.[8]

The G.P.C.C. and Gujarat politics revolved round Vallabhbhai and his hold was complete. By 1921 the role was reversed. Gandhi sought the advice of Vallabhbhai in matters of Gujarat virtually relinquished. Vallabhbhai became its sole leader. Patel and Yagnik, who both belonged to Kaira district, could not get along well. Yagnik wanted Congress to devolve more funds for uplifting tribes and untouchables. He wanted sufficient money to carry relief operation among Bhils in Panchmahal during famine. But much to his dismay Patel could not divert fund. Yagnik had to resign. Gandhi accepted the resignation of Yagnik. He preferred Vallabhbhai a skilful organizer and man of diplomatic manoeuvring.[9]

G.P.C.C. workers, volunteers, local link leaders from village, *Taluka*, district and province were asked to organize the all India level first Non-Cooperation Movement. It was decided to select Bardoli *Taluka* in Surat district, South Gujarat as a unit of Non-Cooperation

Movement. Gandhi gave slogan, ***"Swaraj within an year if people abide by his four point political programme - boycott of British goods, government jobs, recruitment in the army, boycott of government schools, colleges and honorary titles, degrees, adoption of Swadeshi, Khadi, spinning, prohibition"*** etc.

The local workers of Surat district enthusiastically adopted Gandhi's programme. But again the second led Gandhi movement failed miserably. The movement before got momentum was withdrawn on the pretext of Chauri Chaura's violent incident in U.P. In fact Bardoli *Taluka* lacked preparation and provided sufficient ground to withdraw movement. The 60 per cent of *Taluka*'s tribal population was ignorant of the movement. The success of Gandhian movement envisaged the support of all sections of the people. Gandhi found the body polity of the *Taluka* paralytic. He asked G.P.C.C. grass-root workers to infuse blood in the *Taluka*. As a result, unit of six *Ashram* Organization was started in the tribal area of South Gujarat Vallabhbhai became the President of *Swaraj Ashram Sangh* founded at Surat as an Umbrella Organization.[10]

Vallabhbhai made constructive programme the core programme on the agenda of the G. P. C. C. if party at all was to form credible parallel government. The basic concept was to provide service to the people. He gradually united leaders of higher level, local leaders, workers and volunteers. All piped together to constitute homogeneous structure. His workers served the people during influenza, plague epidemics and famines. In 1927, due to excessive rain many rivers in Gujarat were in spate. The thousands of villages were marooned. He undertook, rescue operation on military line, women were the main plank to carry constructive programme of spinning, selling of *Khadi*, prohibition and education. He created a band of workers ready to respond his clarion call for political mass action.[11]

Patel could earn credentials as a master Organizer and great party leader. This success was due to his closely-knit contact, with industrialists and businessmen. He had guts to secure funds for the party as well as to carry relief works across Gujarat. As a hard realist he owed no allegiance to vague ideologies. He refused to subscribe to the radical doctrine that all private property and all profits were immoral.[12]

Vallabhbhai Patel As A Mass Mobilizer

Vallabhbhai faced unwelcome shifts and structural weaknesses in the congress party in Gujarat when Gandhi withdrew the first historic Non-Co-operation Movement in 1922. The Gujarat Congress responded sharply in consonance with the national level development. It also divided in the no changers who had faith in Gandhian technique and changer who had lost faith in Gandhi. Vallabhbhai tried his level best to stop divisions he adhered to Gandhian ideology while his brother Vithalbhai not.

Patel constantly grappled with the modus operandi of Gandhi and realized its limitation of lack of practical application. Patel a man of intense application decided to make the passive resistance a success.[13]

Vallabhbhai got the opportunity to lead Nagpur Flag *Satyagraha* in Madhya Pradesh in 1923. The task was more difficult. He was a man of crystal clear mind and could see core problem without losing time. Patel sent the group of volunteers from almost all the major towns of Gujarat. Vallabhbhai himself led the procession flagrantly violated Government orders against using Congress flag in procession.

Again in the same year in October 1923 he won another milestone. He successfully launched Borsad and Ras *Satyagraha* in his hometowns against the Governor's unjust imposition of punitive tax to curb outlaw with great efficiency. He created homogeneous structure by mobilizing masses through caste councils and village panchayats. He raised also the instrument of social boycott against taxpayers.

By leading two successful campaigns he could show *Satyagraha* in action. He secured break through. He revoked the faith in passive resistance and Gandhian ideology not only with the Congress but in the minds of people also. The presence of Gandhi was no longer needed. Gandhi was worshipped as saintly figure. Vallabhbhai earned the popular credential the '*Suba*' of Gujarat.

By this time Vallabhbhai Patel came to be known as skilful organizer, indefatigable campaigner and shrewd calculating negotiator.[14]

The year 1928 proved to be a watershed for Vallabhbhai. He was called upon to lead Bardoli peasant agitation in Surat district in South Gujarat against Government proposal of steep rise of 22 per cent land revenue as revised rates. He brought the movement to its successful logical end. The Government had to keen the land revenue to rise only by six per cent.[15]

The Bardoli peasant campaign proved to be the classic of Gandhian *Satyagraha* and unique example of amalgamation of urban, rural mass. It again reinforces people's faith and *Satyagraha* became the potent force after Bardoli ***"Let us Bardolize our agitation"*** was the most popular slogan throughout the country. Under the Presidency of Vallabhbhai All Presidency Land League was formed. Congress could create a powerful lobby of supportive peasants. The whole nation honoured him as ***"Sardar"*** [Commander]. The Calcutta Congress passed the resolution to that effect.

While the apostle of *Satyagraha* technique Mahatma Gandhi failed, Vallabhbhai his disciple made it a grand success. Later on, Gandhi accepted that Vallabhbhai as a master organizer made *ahimsa* a reality put into action. Why did Vallabhbhai succeed while Gandhi failed? The answer is the following chart suggests how Vallabhbhai could secure cohesive structure of the movement avoiding disruptions and flaws:

A Model Chart[16]

Satyagraha In Action Aimed At Homogeneous Organisational Structure

1. Selection of unit of Civil Disobedience Movement District or *Taluka*.
2. Division of villages of the district or *Taluka* into various camps.
3. Selection of head quarter of the camp on strategic, geo-political and socio-ethnic considerations.

Camps

5 or 7 10 or 14 15 or 8 or 2

Cluster of villages

Power structure of Camps: 1: Division Leader
2: 5 to 7 Local leaders
3: About 100 volunteers.

4. Total Power structure of the movement.
   1. First Echelon Leadership under Gandhi or Vallabhbhai Patel.
   2. Second Echelon leadership of Camp or Division leader. They were drawn from various parts of Gujarat. They were highly experienced and stood in high esteem. They had to organize, guide and channelize the energy of masses into non-

violent action. They were to remain constantly into dialogue with higher authority and also with local leaders.

3. Local - grass-root workers.
4. Band of volunteers: They remained about 1500. They provided intelligence service. They were mostly young students.

5. Process of mobilisation:

Vertical Mobilisation *Horizontal Mobilisation of society*

Under National Division Leader or according to caste and communities

bringing various caste communities and class in to one umbrella.

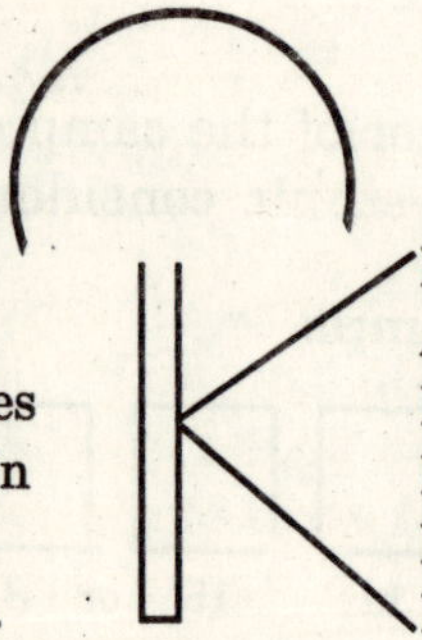

Patidar
Anavil
Baniya :
Brahmins
Muslims
Parsis

through Respective Women Leaders

Tribals

Tools

1. Organizational network
2. Mass Media Publications of Journal Magazines, *Patrikas*.
3. Public meetings, procession
4. *Bhajan Mandlis, Bhuwas*.

Sardar Vallabhbhai Patel again organized 'Quit India Movement' in Gujarat on sound footings in 1942. Nowhere else it was well organized. It became nerve centre and volatile cauldron; it surpassed all the Congress led movements in its level of mass participation. The large number of urban as well as rural based peasants took part in the guerrilla style of attack on Government property - the symbol of imperial and colonial regime.

The Congress geared up its machinery in Gujarat, Vallabhbhai travelled far and wide during the months of June and July 1942. The fear of Japanese invasion was looming large. The rumour was strong. The British would leave us in larch as they did in Singapore and Malaysia. He wanted to make Gujarat the epicentre of the ensuing movement. He organized public meetings, met cross section of people, and activated organizations, asked industrialists, merchants, workers, peasants, leaders, and volunteers to be ready to strike. On 2, July, 1942 at Surat he said, ***"This will not be along struggle. It must produce quick results. We must get independence before the Japanese come here".*** On another occasion he stated, ***"Do not wait for any programme. This is the last battle of our life, invent your own programme. There is no time for jail going"*** on 25th July, 1942 he called Provincial Congress Committee meeting, while explaining the situation, he said point blank, ***"The Congress would not interfere if some people lost their temper and took drastic steps against the government during the struggle".*** He added, ***"Incidents like Chauri-Chaura would not deter Congress".*** He covertly and overtly approved violence. Kishorlal Mashruwala, a staunch Gandhian wrote in September, 1942 an article in Harijan Bandhu under the heading, ***"Do not talk, and quickly act".*** Patel went to Bombay to prepare for AICC meeting where the famous Quit India Resolution was passed on 8 August 1942.[17]

The news of the arrest of Gandhi, Vallabhbhai and all rank and file leaders of the Congress spread like wide fire. The people became furious; the 1942 movement surpassed in its level of anti-British sentiments. The mill workers downed their tools, the students left their schools and colleges, the merchants downed the shutters, the business came to a virtual halt. It was a perfect case of mass mobilization.[18]

Vallabhbhai could successfully neutralize the socialists group that developed within the Congress in Gujarat. He also tried his level best to keep *Kisan Sabha* movement of landless peasants within a circumscribed nature. In the emergence of Vallabhbhai Patel as a national leader the people of Gujarat played Key role and vice-a-versa.

References

1. Rajmohan Gandhi, Patel: A Life, [Navajivan, Ahmedabad, 1990] p. 41.
2. Narhari Parikh, *Sardar Vallabhbhai Patel,* [Ahmedabad, 1953] Vol. 1, p. 18.
3. Shirin Mehta, *Peasantry and Nationalism: A Case Study of Bardoli Satyagraha*, [New Delhi, 1884] p. 29.
4. *Ibid.*, p. 76.
5. *Ibid.*, p. IV.
6. David Hardiman, *Peasant Nationalists of Gujarat Kaira District 1971-1984.*
7. Author's Interview with Kunwerji Mehta.
8. Shankerlal Dwarkadas Parikh, *Khedani Ladat* [in Gujarat], [Ahmedabad, 1923], p. 89.
9. Indulal Yagnik, *Atma Katha* [Ahmedabad, 1970], Part IV, p. 106.
10. Shirin Mehta, *Peasantry*, p. 106.
11. Howard Spodek, 'Gandhi's Political Methodology', The Journal of Asian Studies [Michigan], Volume 33, No. 2, 3 February 1971, pp. 365-77.
12. Bipin Chandra, 'Sardar Patel: A Re-Evaluation' in Bipin Chandra, *Essays on Indian Nationalism,* [New Delhi, 1993] pp. 169-190.
13. Author's Interview with Kalyanji Mehta.

14. Abdul Majid Khan, Life and Speeches of Sardar Patel, [Delhi, 1951] p. 131.
15. Shirin Mehta, Peasantry, pp. 173-85.
16. *Ibid.*, p. 110-116.
17. Shirin Mehta, 'Peasant's Assertion in Gujarat and Quit India Movement of 1942', *Samipya,* April 91-March 1992, pp. 74-80.
18. David Hardiman, 'Quit India Movement in Gujarat' Gyandev Pandya Ed; *The Indian*
19. *Nation in 1942* K.P. Bagahi, [Calcutta, 1988], pp. 78-121.

15

Sardar Vallabhbhai Patel and Merger of the State of Hyderabad

B. Satyanarayan Reddy

I was 19 years old when the independence of India was declared. Since 1942, other than my studies, I used to take part in political activities. At that time political activities were not as open in the Hyderabad State as was in the rest of India. It was under the rule of the Nizam and the organization of the Congress was not strong there. The political awareness was also not seen on a large scale and the awareness that was seen there it was due to the work done by the '*Arya Samaj*.'

When the last Viceroy and the Governor-General of India, Lord Mountbatten, announced independence for India, our hearts were filled with joy. Especially the youth of the State became full of enthusiasm. But our joy suffered a major shock when the Nizam of Hyderabad declared a separate identity of his State. This meant that the people of Hyderabad State could not be able to enjoy the right of freedom as the rest of the Indians.

Under the policy of separatism, the officials of Nizam started making large scale arresting of the people who demanded democracy in the State. The Congress was banned in the State. Its all prominent leaders like, Swami Ramananda Tirtha, Digambar Rao Bindu, B. Ramakrishna Rao, etc., were also arrested. My young companions and I myself were put behind the bar.

A state of unrest emerged in the Hyderabad State. Not only this, communal activities also started disturbing the State. The target to those communal atrocities was not only the Hindu majority but also the nationalist Muslims. What would happen to the people of Hyderabad State? Until when would the atrocities and communalism affect the peace of the State? Would the State remain separate from the Union of India or whether it would remain different from other States? These were some crucial questions at that time. In jail we kept on thinking in this regard. We also held discussion on the ways to free the State from communalism, atrocities and dictatorship.

As in jail we used to get information occasionally from the statements and the intention of Sardar Patel, who being the Home Minister of India was also the Minister in charge for the State affairs, which he had regarding Princely States; so we started believing strongly that one day the Hyderabad State would merge in the Union of India. Especially, the first and general statement issued by Sardar Patel regarding the policy towards Princely States and then the statement issued in October 1947 particularly about the Hyderabad State, made the things very clear. Sardar Patel said:

"If Hyderabad is to be saved, it must effect a radical change in its methods and policy. In the world of today, only those who have guts can make their voice felt. If Hyderabad wishes to be heard, it must follow bravely and courageously the popular will. Otherwise, Hyderabad's fate will sooner or

later be the same as those of other Rulers and dynasties who had attempted to thwart the popular will only at the cost of their existence."

Due to the constant efforts and clear policy of Sardar Patel, the Hyderabad State finally merged into the Union of India. In the whole course of events, Sardar Patel showed an astounding patience and yet kept making efforts due to his firm determination. This was the reason that when no other option was left, he took military action to bring the State out of turmoil. This was totally justified and was in the interest of the innocent people of the State.

After military action, the State was freed from the claws of communal and anti-social elements like Qasim Rizvi. A responsible government was formed in the State. More than 10 million people got the right to decide their own fate. This was a great task and all the credit of it goes to Sardar Vallabhbhai Patel. This is the reason that I call him the greatest of the leaders.

Sardar Patel was a leader of a unique and strong will power. He had a clear view-point. He never accessed an issue religiously. When he ordered military action in Hyderabad, some people tried to call it a communal action. But the action was successful and after sometime, Sardar Patel reached Hyderabad. The speech he delivered at the city, made things clear for everyone. His speech was to call everyone on the basis of compassion, harmony and unity. He said:

"We have to create conditions in which Hindus and Muslims can live amicably together. Especially in Hyderabad, I want to say, let us bury the past. The clean thing is to purge our hearts of animosity, now that we have broadly achieved what we wanted. It is cowardice to hit a fallen person. We should rather give him a helping hand and lift him up.

The Muslims here are not foreigners. They are from among ourselves. We should unite Hindus and Muslims."

As the Nizam had taken a stand opposite to India, he had challenged the Indian Union by declaring to remain separate. Therefore, after military action, a demand was made that the Nizam should be punished. But Sardar Patel treated the Nizam with compassion. The Nizam was appointed the Constitutional Head of the State. Those who were suspected of Sardar Patel came to know of the reality through this action.

There is no doubt that Sardar Patel was a great man. I render my thousand salutations to his greatness.

16

SARDAR PATEL: A TRUE GANDHIAN

Paitoon Patyaiying

Sardar Vallabhbhai Patel was a great and popular leader of the Indian Sub-continent. His personality was constituted with the qualities of self-confidence, truthfulness, strength and non-violence. On the basis of these qualities, he emerged as a unique and true Gandhian of his time. Not only this, but in reality it seems that till now there has not been another Gandhian in India, who could equal him.

The first proof of his being a Gandhian is seen during the Kaira Satyagraha of 1918. This *Satyagraha* was started under the leadership of Mahatma Gandhi to bring justice to the farmers. The manner, in which Sardar Vallabhbhai Patel worked day and night for the *Satyagraha*, was the main reason for its success. For this very reason, after the success of this *Satyagraha*, Mahatma Gandhi said that if he had not met Vallabhbhai Patel then the things that have achieved, could not be achieved.[1]

The second important and authentic proof of Sardar Patel being a Gandhian comes to light in the year 1922.

This was the time when Mahatma Gandhi had called off the Non-Cooperation Movement after the violent incident at Chauri-Chaura. After the calling off the movement, a group inside the Indian National Congress itself had started questioning Mahatma Gandhi's principle of Non-Violence. Not only this but that group also remarked that Mahatma Gandhi's philosophy was irrelevant so some other option should be sought. In such a critical time, Sardar Vallabhbhai Patel defended Mahatma Gandhi's philosophy in just the same manner as once done by Lenin for Marxism early in the twentieth century. In this reference, Prof. N.G. Ranga had justly said:

"By doing so, Sardar Vallabhbhai Patel established himself as a great Gandhian."[2]

Several *Satyagrahas*, especially the records established during the Bardoli *Satyagraha*, prove Sardar Vallabhbhai Patel to be a unique Gandhian. If he had not been a great Gandhian, then the manner in which he attained success on the basis of Non-Violence, in the Bardoli *Satyagraha*, had never been possible.

India is a very big country and it was not easy to unify more than five hundred Princely States under one central rule. But on the basis of cooperation, goodwill and compromise, Sardar Vallabhbhai Patel was able to unify all of them into one Union of India in a short period of time. History is the witness of his noble task. Still, this great task was accomplished because Sardar Vallabhbhai Patel was a true and practical Gandhian.

There cannot be any doubt in Sardar Vallabhbhai Patel's being a true Gandhian. He believed in action and not merely in philosophy. This is the sign of a true Gandhian. Still if someone has a doubt on Sardar Vallabhbhai Patel, then he should take into notice his own words:

"I have locked myself up and given the key to Mahatma Gandhi."

We know that several people, working under the leadership of Mahatma Gandhi, tried to become Gandhian. Also some among them were considered to be great Gandhian but to fully devote his actions according to the guidance of Mahatma Gandhi was only one - Sardar Vallabhbhai Patel. This was and is, the fact proving Sardar Vallabhbhai Patel to be a true and unique Gandhian.

References

1. Young India, [A weekly, edited by M. K. Gandhi], 1918, Navajivan Press, Ahmedabad [Gujarat, India].
2. Prof. Ranga further said: ***"By becoming the political follower of Gandhiji and by giving up his legal practice and by ably promoting the non-cooperation and triple boycott programme and by sticking loyally along with Rajaji [C. Rajagopalachari] to the Gandhian line in opposition to Motilal Nehru and C. R. Das's deviation in favour of Council entry, Vallabhbhai established his reputation as the most dependable disciple of Gandhiji".***

17

SARDAR PATEL – ARCHITECT OF UNITY AND INTEGRITY

P. P. Rao

Vallabhbhai Patel was a prosperous lawyer when he joined the Freedom Movement inspired by Mohandas Karamchand Gandhi. In the words of P.N. Haksar, ***"Sardar Patel was one of the remarkable men thrown up by the turbulence which Mahatma Gandhi generated in the hearts of the Indian people."***[1] Very soon he emerged as a leader of local self-government in Ahmedabad. His qualities of leadership came to light during the Bardoli *Satyagraha* – a massive protest by the peasants. He successfully organized Civil Disobedience and no-tax campaign that paralysed the administration in Bardoli. The people spontaneously hailed him as ***'Sardar'*** [born leader]. Gandhiji utilized his organizational skills for strengthening the Indian National Congress. Sardar Patel enjoyed the confidence of the Congress cadres all over the country and rose to become President of the party. But for Gandhiji's preference for Nehru, Patel could have in all probability become the Prime Minister of India.

As Deputy Prime Minister in Jawaharlal Nehru's Cabinet, Sardar Patel's achievements were unparalleled.

Being an astute administrator, he did not hesitate to deploy Armed Forces to bring Nizam's dominion into the Indian Union. He brought about integration of hundreds of Princely States with the rest of India and made united India a reality. Justice P.B. Gajendragadkar, former Chief Justice of India, spoke of Patel's diplomacy and tact, his persuasiveness and imagination in accomplishing the task. Gajendragadkar called him a Maker of Modern India.[2] Speaking of Sardar Patel, C. Rajagopalachari observed: ***"It was said of Augustus that it would have been better for Rome if Augustus had never been born or had never died. This can be said with great truth about India and Vallabhbhai Patel."***.[3]

In the words of Dr. Zakir Hussain:

"Sardar was a valiant fighter for the country's freedom and as a great builder of its future greatness on the firm foundations of an integrated political structure."[4]

Dr. Tara Chand says: ***"of the men who guided the destinies of India after the achievement of independence in 1947, Sardar Vallabhbhai Patel, aptly called the man of iron, was one of those distinguished statesmen who accomplished tasks of lasting value for the future of the country."***[5]

Frank Moraes compared him with Bismarck who had unified Germany.[6]

To K.P.S. Menon, a distinguished diplomat and a prolific writer, Patel was like ***"a flame in windless spot which does not flicker"*** and ***"essentially a man of action, not of words."***[7]

Very few people are lucky to realize their cherished dreams in their lifetime. Sardar Patel was one such. He wanted India to be free, strong and united. He worked for it and succeeded substantially. Had he been given a free hand, he would have settled the Kashmir dispute on Indian soil in the very first instance instead of taking the issue to the United Nations. The people of Jammu & Kashmir would have been spared of so much of agony and suffering for so long. Pakistan would have been put in its place. As Independent India's first Minister of Information & Broadcasting, Sardar Patel acting as a link with the national goals and objectives of the freedom movement, initiated idealization of the Government - controlled media and the processes of drawing communication network – especially All India Radio and Information Departments – into the mainstream of nation-building.[8]

Another achievement of Sardar Patel was retention of the services of civil servants who had served the British rulers with admirable devotion. He realized the need for an organized, efficient, disciplined and contented service with assured prospects, conscious of its duty to serve independent India with diligent and honest work and persuaded them to continue in service. The civil servants including members of the prestigious Indian Civil Service acted on the advice of Patel and gave their best to independent India. The administration was strong, efficient and free from corruption. They maintained the traditional neutrality and served their new masters and the people of India with equal devotion, if not more. It is because of the efficient administrative machinery in position, the initial decades following independence were an era of consolidation, development and achievement.

Constitution-making is always a challenging task. The contribution made by Sardar Patel in this area is equally profound. In February, 1947, the Advisory Committee on Minorities and Fundamental Rights constituted by the Constituent Assembly unanimously elected Sardar Patel as its Chairman. Sardar Patel had confessed in the Assembly that he was ***'trembling'*** on the day he was appointed as Chairman of this Committee. He had taken up the job with ***"a heavy heart"***, because he felt that the task was immensely difficult, owing to the history of the past through so many years of foreign rule. The conditions of the country were extremely difficult and all classes of people were full of misgivings and suspicion. He felt, however, that with the transfer of power a gradual transformation had begun and there was a ***"gradual growth of trust and mutual confidence".***[9] He approached the work of the Committee in a spirit of helpful understanding. On that occasion, he told the Committee:

"Nobody can be more interested than us in India in the protection of our minorities. Our mission is to satisfy every one of them and we hope we shall be able to satisfy every interest and safeguard the interests of all the minorities to their satisfaction. Let us hope that our deliberations will be so conducted that we can disillusion those who are looking with a critical eye outside... we know how to rule better than those who claim that they can rule others... in this committee, therefore, we begin our work today with a determination and a desire to come to decisions not by majority but by uniformity. Let us sink all our differences and look to one and one interest only, which is the interest of all of us – the interest of India as a whole."[10]

In April, 1947 presenting the interim report of the Advisory Committee on Fundamental Rights to the President of the Constituent Assembly, he mentioned:

"We are of the opinion that Fundamental rights of the citizens of the Union would have no value if they differed from group to group or unit to unit or are not uniformly enforceable."[11]

Submitting the report of the Advisory Committee on Minority Rights in August, 1947, he observed: ***"by an*** *overwhelming majority, we came to the conclusion that the system of separate electorates must be abolished in the new constitution. In our judgment, this system has in the past, sharpened communal differences to a dangerous extent and has proved one of the main stumbling blocks to the development of a healthy national life. It seems specially necessary to avoid these dangers in the new political conditions that have developed in the country and from this point of view the arguments against separate electorates seem to us absolutely decisive."*[12]

While moving the report of the Advisory committee on Minorities for consideration by the Constituent Assembly on August 27, 1947, he said :

"It may be that there are some who are not satisfied on some points, but we have to take into consideration all points of view and feelings and sentiments of the minorities, big and small. We have tried as far as possible to meet the wishes of all the minorities. The minorities among themselves are also divided; there are conflicting interests among them. We have not tried to take advantage of these differences among the minorities themselves; we have tried to see that the minorities also instead of being divided among themselves try to present a united front in order to safeguard their interests. But there are certain points on which the minorities cannot be united because there are minorities within minorities. So it is a difficult proposition. We have tried to solve this difficult problem without any bitterness and without any controversy which would create any ill feeling or hitch." [13]

He showed a remarkable understanding of the sensitivities of the minorities when he referred to the Sikh community on May 25, 1949 and observed:

"The Sikhs today, it should be recognized have suffered from various causes and we have to regard

with considerable tenderness of feeling in taking into consideration their state of mind and provide as far as possible to meet with that situation.".[14]

He paid a compliment to the Parsi community and said:

"It is well known that though small, it is very powerful community and perhaps very wise. They know that any concession that they may get would perhaps do more harm to them than any good, because they can make their way anywhere, and make their way in such a manner that they would get more than they would get by any reservation or by any separate process of elections. Either in the legislatures or in the services, they stand so high in the general standard of the nation that they have disclaimed any concessions and I congratulate them on their decision."[15]

Dealing with the concessions to Schedules Caste Sikhs, he said: *"Now our object is, or the object of this House should be as soon as possible and as rapidly as possible to drop these classifications and differences and bring all to a level of equality. Therefore, although temporarily we may recognize this, it is up to the majority community to create by its generosity a sense of confidence in the minorities; and so also it will be a duty of the minority communities to forget the past and to reflect on what the country has suffered due to sense of fairness which the foreigner thought was necessary to keep the balance between community and community. This has created class and communal divisions and sub-divisions, which in their sense of fairness they thought fit to create, apart from attributing any motives. We on our part, taking this responsibility of laying the foundations of a free India which shall be and should be our endeavour both of the majority–*

***largely of the majority – and also of the minority community, have to rise to the situation that is demanded from all of us, and create an atmosphere in which the sooner these classifications disappear the better."*[16]**

Speaking generally about the minorities including Muslims, he said, ***"It is not our intention to commit the minorities to a particular position in a hurry. If they really have come honestly to the conclusion that in the changed conditions of this country, it is in the interest of all to lay down real and genuine foundations of a secular State, then nothing is better for the minorities than to trust the good-sense and sense of fairness of the majority, and to place confidence in them. So also it is for us who happen to be in a majority to think about what the minorities feel, and how we in their position would feel if we were treated in the manner in which they are treated. But in the long run, it would be in the interest of all to forget that there is anything like majority or minority in this country and that in India there is only one community."*[17]**

In May 1947, Sardar Patel was unanimously elected Chairman of the Provisional Constitution Committee. Moving the report of the Committee in the Constituent Assembly on July 15, 1947, he commended the Parliamentary system as in Britain as best suited to India with which they were familiar.[18] The Committee took the view that as the authority of the administration entirely vests in the Ministry, the Governor could be given a limited power of reporting to the President of the Union. Regarding appointment of Judges of High Court, he said: ***"this is considered to be very important by the Committee and as the judiciary should be above suspicion and should be above party influences, it was agreed that the appointment of***

High Court Judges should be made by the President of the Union in consultation with the Chief Justice of the Supreme Court, the Chief Justice of the Provincial High Court and the Governor with the advice of the Ministry of the Province concerned. So, there are many checks provided to ensure fair appointments to the High Court."[19]

After accomplishing the task of integration of States, Sardar Patel highlighted the basic conception underlying the new Constitution of India – that Provinces and States are equal partners. He observed: ***"All the citizens of India, whether residing in States or Provinces, will enjoy the same fundamental rights and the same legal remedies to enforce them. In the matter of their constitutional relationship with the Centre and in their internal set-up, the States will be on a par with the Provinces... Our new Constitution is not an alliance between democracies and dynasties, but really a union of the Indian people built on the basic concept of sovereignty of the people. It removes all barriers between the people of the States and the people of Provinces and achieves for the first time the objective of a strong democratic India built on the true foundation of a cooperative enterprise on the part of the people of the Provinces and States alike."***[20]

Adverting to the political and moral aspect of the settlements made with the Rulers of the States including Privy Purse, he observed: ***"In order to view the payments guaranteed by us in their correct perspective, we have to remember that they are linked with the momentous developments affecting the most vital interests of this country. These guarantees form part of the historic settlements which enshrine in them the consummation of the great ideal of geographical, political and economic unification of India, an ideal***

which for centuries remained a distant dream and which appeared as remote and as difficult of attainment as even after the advent of Indian independence." [21]

He explained that in view of the freedom given to the States to link their future with whichever dominion they liked and wish of some of the Rulers to exercise their technical right to declare independence and others to join the neighbouring dominion, the situation was indeed fraught with immeasurable potentialities of disruption. He said: ***"Need we cavil then at the small – I purposely use the word small – price we have paid for bloodless revolution which has affected the destinies of millions of our people. The capacity for mischief and trouble on the part of the Rulers if the settlement with them had not been reached on a negotiated basis was far greater than could be imagined at this stage. Let us do justice to them; let us place ourselves in their position and then assess the value of their sacrifice. The Rulers have now discharged their part of the obligations by transferring all ruling powers and by agreeing to the integration of their States. The main part of our obligation under these agreements is to ensure that the guarantees given by us in respect of privy purses are fully implemented. Our failure to do so would be a breach of faith and seriously prejudice the stabilization of the new order."*** [22]

In 1970 by a Presidential order, the recognition of Rulers was withdrawn in order to deny them the benefit of Privy Purse that Sardar Patel had assured them. However, the Supreme Court quashed the order declaring it ultra virus the Constitution.[23]

The Constituent Assembly would not have had so much of talent, eminence, equipment, wisdom and representative character but for the farsightedness of the Congress leaders of the day. They wanted to frame a modern constitution based on liberal values and with social objectives, which would endure for ages. For accomplishing this stupendous task, they needed to bring in all leaders of eminence and experience from different walks of public life including men and women who would not have otherwise cared to subject themselves to the uncertainties of the electoral process. Mahatma Gandhi, Pandit Jawaharlal Nehru, Sardar Vallabhbhai Patel, Maulana Azad, Babu Rajendra Prasad, C. Rajagopalachari and others rose above party politics and saw to it that a galaxy of prominent citizens got elected as members of the great Assembly, the like of which is not witnessed again and not likely to be seen in the foreseeable future. B. Shiva Rao himself a distinguished member of the Constituent Assembly and brother of Sir B. N. Rao, the Constitution Advisor, recounts: ***"A member of the Congress Party asked the Sardar with a sense of grievance: Why was Dr. Ambedkar, who had been a bitter critic of Gandhiji and an opponent of the Congress Party, chosen to be the Chairman of the Drafting Committee?."***

The Sardar's reply was characteristic, ***"What do you know of Constitution-making?" and added, "We have chosen the best man for the job."*** Shiva Rao says: ***"whenever the Drafting Committee found it difficult to convince a member or a group of members in the party – and such occasions were many – of its considered view on a particular question, a meeting was usually arranged at the residence of the Sardar, and the differences were quickly resolved."***[24]

The country is indebted to leaders like Sardar Patel who had sacrificed their all in the Freedom movement and worked hard after Independence to lay strong foundations of unity and integrity of India, without misusing their official position for selfish ends.

References

1. Patel Memorial Lecture-1974.
2. Patel Memorial Lecture-1966.
3. Patel Memorial Lecture-1955.
4. Patel Memorial Lecture-1958.
5. Patel Memorial Lecture-1960.
6. "Witness to an Era" [1973] published by Vikas Publishing House Pvt. Ltd., p. 185.
7. Patel Memorial Lecture-1962.
8. P.C. Joshi - Patel Memorial Lecture-1985.
9. B. Shiva Rao's article: "Sardar Patel and the Constitution" published in the compilation "Political Thinkers of Modern India" by Deep & Deep Publications.
10. B. Shiva Rao – "Framing of India's Constitution, Selected Documents" Vol. II p. 66.
11. *Ibid* p. 294.
12. *Ibid* p. 412.
13. *Ibid* p. 423.
14. Constituent Assembly Debates, Vol. VIII p. 271.
15. *Ibid* Vol.V p. 200.
16. *Ibid* Vol.VIII pp. 271-272.
17. *Ibid* p. 272.
18. *Ibid* Vol.IV p. 578.
19. *Ibid* Vol.IV pp. 579-580.
20. *Ibid* Vol.X pp. 163-164.
21. *Ibid* pp. 166-167.
22. *Ibid* p. 167.
23. Madhav Rao Jiwajirao Scindia v. Union of India [1971] 3 SCR 9 = [1971] 1 SCC 85 = AIR 1971 SC 530.
24. B. Shiva Rao's article "Sardar Patel and the Constitution" *op cit* pp.399-400.

18

THE PATH SHOWN BY SARDAR PATEL

Sachin Bathla

The first President of India, Dr. Rajendra Prasad, in his funeral speech in Mumbai, on the 15th of December 1950 said about Sardar Vallabhbhai Patel:

"Sardar's body is being consumed by fire; but no fire on earth can consume his fame. The earthly body of Sardar Patel has gone. But in the form of the services he has rendered to his country, he would live for all time. Those left behind would have to continue the work left by him unfinished."

Even after 53 years of the death of Sardar Vallabhbhai Patel, the truth of Dr. Rajendra Prasad's above statement stands unchanged. Still it reminds us of Sardar Patel's great and noble works and calls upon us Indians to step forward on the simple but straight pathway of national Integrity and social development.

Sardar Patel remained active in public life for a period of about 33 years [1917-1950]. In these 33 years, from a freedom fighter, he achieved the status of the

Commander of the Indian struggle for freedom or we can say that from a worker, he became a leader and from a *Satyagrahi*, he emerged as a great statesman. The manner in which he held direct and close contacts with leaders, workers and general public alike, had always been the prime reason of his astounding success.

By maintaining direct and close contacts, Sardar Patel had been able to unite thousands and millions of people into one unified community that could stand against the Imperial rule, in the struggle for independence. Later, when India became free from the shake of imperialistic rule, several problems hurdled the pathway of our country. These problems included communalism, regionalism, provincialism, racial segregation, etc. Not only this but some anti-national and anti-social elements had started emerging in some parts of the country. In such a situation, Sardar Patel called upon the people to forget their differences and once again get united to fight against such elements. His call received a very good response from people and they stepped ahead. Thus, one after the other, the nation started recovering from the problems.

Whether it was the *Majlis-I-Ittehad-Ul-Musalmeen*, a communal organization of Hyderabad or the Muslim National *Guardo* and *Khaskaro*; whether it were the anti-social elements of Telangana region or of Kerala; all were crushed until they lost their hopes. It was but natural that Sardar Patel, with the support of masses, had taken strict measures for their eradication.

He once said:

"We are not going to let the grass grow under our feet. Even if all these troubles come at the same time, we have got resources which would enable us to stand up to all of them at the same time. If they are anxious to challenge us, we would be ready to

accept it. Let no one have evil designs on us or dream of extending its hegemony. Let them not entertain the fond hope of any Jatistan or Rajasthan or Sikhistan...”

Sardar Patel had a unique quality of getting support from all and uniting them together to work for the cause of the nation. On the basis of this great quality, he was able to succeed in a near impossible task of the Unification of India and later paved the way for India's development in all fields. He could fill people with courage and confidence and as such was able to inspire people to accomplish such tasks.

Even today, his inspiration is alive and will remain alive in the hearts of millions of Indians who are committed for national development, unity and integrity.

Rajaji has stated justly:

“What inspiration, courage, confidence and force incarnate Vallabhbhai was! The real Vallabhbhai has survived, even after the Vallabhbhai we knew, breathed last.”

Even today, the path shown by Sardar Patel is simple. If we have the strong desire for the prosperity of our country, if we feel the need for real development of our nation, then we should constantly walk ahead on the path shown by Sardar Patel. But we need to be duty bound for the strengthening of our country by establishing internal unity.

19

Sardar Patel: National Unity and Integrity

Anjula Rajvanshi

"History has examples of conquerors who carved out empires with the might of their sward. It has instances of man rising in revolt, overthrowing established regimes, creating new states by breaking up existing ones. But not once in history has an individual managed to transform the shape of a vast country like India through a process of negotiation, persuasion and accommodation. The credit goes to Sardar Patel." -D. V. T.

Sardar Patel, known as Iron Man of India was committed to national unity and integrity. He was a peace-loving person, a great freedom fighter, devoted to communal harmony, a God fearing person, a fearless believing in non-violence, not only in theory, but [also] in practice. Discipline, simplicity and nationalism were the main characteristics of his life. He was among those few who loved India from the core of their hearts and sacrificed their entire lives for the cause of the nation. Moreover, endurance, forbearance and tolerance were the parts of nationalism. He was a true Indian who tried to remove contempt from every mind and suggested:

"A State should avoid the discrimination of cast, creed and religion..."

As a leader of the masses, Sardar Vallabhbhai Patel desired to step ahead on the path of progress so that India could achieve some great heights. He urged the people to make India a united, consolidated and peaceful nation free from internal disturbances and communalism. Especially, for the solution of the problem of communalism in India Sardar Patel rightly advised:

"Communal problem should be solved keeping the welfare of the country in mind."

After a continuous ninety years' struggle for freedom by Indians, Lord Mountbatten in his authority of British Viceroy and Governor-General, declared independence and partition of India on June 3, 1947. With the partition of India a new nation namely Pakistan also came into being. As the formation of Pakistan was based on demand of homeland for the followers of a particular religion, it gave rise to many disheartened events. A wave of communalism, groupism, frustration and violence overwhelmed India and Pakistan. In such a serious situation, Sardar Vallabhbhai Patel, in his authority of the Deputy Prime Minister and Minister of Home Affairs, India, undertook the task of maintaining peace and creating [an] atmosphere of harmony. In this regard he asked his countrymen to have confidence and trust and also to understand their responsibilities. If all worked in this spirit then, in Sardar Patel's words:

"I am sure that if we approach the present situation in this spirit and if we discharge to the full obligation which we have incurred under a sense of national honour and prestige, we shall have our part in a big-hearted attempt to heal the wounds and to reserve the process of misunderstanding and bitterness which have unfortunately marred our relationship..."[1]

Not only this, Sardar Patel asked the people to live unite and to go ahead on the path of development collectively. To quote from one of his messages that he conveyed soon after the partition of the country:

"It is difficult to live alone in this world. An isolated tree cannot withstand the storm, but in a group, it can preserve its identity. Because of our welfare, we should be united; otherwise, there will be disaster everywhere."[2]

For the unification and integration of India, Sardar Patel on the hand took the path of harmony, love and non-violence and on the other he took recourse of diplomacy in his dealings with some States like Jaisalmer, Jodhpur and Bikaner. Thus, he unified more than 550 States into the Union of India in a brief period. He was committed to unite India, but on solid basis. And he did so. In his own words:

"We do not want the unity which can break off by a small reason. We want concrete and hearted unity. In present circumstances it can be possible only when all big try to become small."[3]

The merger of the States into the Indian Union was a stupendous achievement. But for Sardar Patel's dynamic drive, unification of the country would still be little more than an ideal to cherish and strive for. The realization of that ideal, according to Tahmankar, ***'has enabled India to speak in one voice and act as guide and mentor to the great majority of uncommitted Afro-Asian countries.'***[4] Unification of India was, thus, a fundamental revolution which created a new world of political relations.

Sardar Patel was an outspoken man and he could not tolerate any hurdle in the way of national unity and integrity. To ensure national unity and integrity was the responsibility of each and every one. He called upon every citizen to be faithful to his nation. And if someone failed to defend his country or tried to be disloyal, he, in the Sardar's view, had no right to stay in the country.

If we go in depth of Sardar's life, views and works, we will find a great social reformer and an educationist in him. He realized that education should be compulsory for all Indians for the betterment not only in the lives of individuals but also for national unity and integrity. He rightly considered education and educators to be the pillars of country's consolidation and asked the teachers to change their views and to take it to be an essential part of their responsibility that every student right from the primary level should be imparted education according to the spirit of nationalism and also [according to] the demand of time and space. In this very context Sardar Patel especially emphasized on change of teacher's attitude and said:

"If your point of view has not changed, you have not guided the student to move forward in right direction, then, they would not be able to become self-dependent. And, thus, the education they would get would be of little use or just waste."

Regarding education, Sardar Vallabhbhai Patel was of the opinion that it is a process which provides ground to a human being for self-dependency. That is why he said:

"To make education worthwhile and young men and women self-dependent through it, we have to make the education fit according to our national circumstances and situation."

Also he advocated of equal opportunities for equal education as far as it is possible. This, according to him, is a step towards the national education.

Sardar Patel believed that it would not be a good sign if the sons of farmers forgot the art of their forefathers; but to bring improvement in the lives of farmers and the method of cultivation according to demand of time was their responsibility. In a country like India where agriculture is at the basis of social and economic structure, if educated young forget the reality, Sardar Patel reminds them to be familiar with it. He also supports indignity, protection to cottage industries on .one hand; asks for industrialization on the other. Without industrialization the talk of development and prosperity of the country would be meaningless. And if country is not prosperous and developed there would be a question mark on its unity and integrity.

Sardar Patel was a mass leader. People all over India loved and respected him. During the migration of population, a group of Muslim refugees going to Pakistan was detained by Sikhs at Amritsar. On this occasion Sardar Patel visited Amritsar and addressing the *Punjabis* said:

"We have got freedom to make our country great and prosperous and not for distorting and devastating what foreign rulers have left for us. If we grow careless, we would not be able to protect our freedom which we have got after so much of struggle and sufferings."

Sardar's appeal left a deep impact on *Punjabis* and they allowed detained Muslims to go by providing a safe passage to them.

For the unity and integrity of the nation, Sardar Patel brought a tremendous reform in the administration. With the consent of provincial governments he also introduced the Indian Administrative Service and the Indian Police Service and tried to make them fit for democratic system. In this regard he asked the people connected with these services to establish close relations with the common men and to work as a chain between the government and the people. As per his advice the people in the administration and the police should consider themselves to be the servant of the people, and not the masters.

For unity and integrity of India, Sardar Patel always emphasized upon discipline and duty. He himself was a duty bound person. His personal life is still a living example of discipline before the nation. If we really want the prosperity of our country, if we desire its long lasting unity and integrity, we need to follow his foot steps even after fifty-four years of his passing away.

References

1. Murti, R. K., Sardar Patel: The Man and His Contemporaries, New Delhi: Sterling Publishers Pvt. Ltd., 1976, p. 36.
2. Kumar, Ravindra, Sardar Patel: Vyaktitva Ke Anchhuye Pahlu [in Hindi], Meerut: Dynamic Publications [India] Ltd., 2003, p. 12-13.
3. *Ibid.*
4. Tahmankar, D. V., Sardar Patel, London: George Allen and Unwin Ltd., 1970, p.19.

20

VALLABH – AS AN INDIVIDUAL

Jayant Oza

Undoubtedly Sardar Patel's most historic achievement was the integration of 564 Princely states with the Union of India. One can not wink at to his concealed foresight to external affairs.

It may be about Tibet-China issue or Nehru's enthusiasm regarding recognition of China in UNO or Indo-China friendship. Sardar has drawn Nehru's attention and even warned him.

My emphasis here is on the few qualities of Sardar as Individual – unbelievable level of tolerance and child care.

When Vallabh was 25 and preparing for pleaders' test, he and his two friends Kashibhai and Chhotabhai were in search of quiet place. They had gone to village Bakrol very near to Karamsad. The place was known as Desai's *Haveli*. Unfortunately, Vallabh developed a boil in his armpit. It was tradition or practice to approach the Barber for removing teeth or puncting boils. The Barber named Madha Rat was summoned. Madha Rat brought his pocker, which he made red hot in a fire in the *Haveli*, but he shrank from taking it to Vallabh's boil. Scolding Madha Rat, Vallabh picked up the pocker and scorched the boil himself. The room - which Vallabh occupied where the incident took place; reached by dark, stiff and narrow staircase – is preserved as memorial.

The glaring and illustrative incident of Vallabh's quality of child care led us to Nadiad. Vallabh was staying and studying at Kashibhai's residence. Kashibhai's father died and friend of father looking after Kashi and Vallabh. This man's wife dies leaving boy of six months. Vallabh takes over the infants' care. He sleeps beside him, feed him milk washes his nappies.

21

Sardar Patel: Administrator And Reformer

Bhupesh Bhatt

Sardar Vallabhbhai Patel was born on the 31st of October 1875, in Gujarat. He was the son of Ladbai and Jhaverbhai, who had served in the army of the Queen of Jhansi. Vallabhbhai started his education in a Gujarati medium school and after middle-school he looked over to English medium [studies] in the Nadiad High School. During the course of his studies his penchant towards organization came to light. He successfully organized many events. As he was born in a village of Central Gujarat and belonged to a humble farmer's family, he could understand the problems and agonies of the farmers of rural India. It was but natural that he was a peasant in his attitude towards life. He lived a simple, disciplined life. His father and brother were all patriots and thus patriotism was his legacy, and not an acquired attribute.

Patel was born and brought up in extremely ordinary circumstances, which made him deeply familiar with adversity and all that it entailed. He thus had direct knowledge of the trials and tribulations of the common man of the land. The taste of adversity perhaps bred in him an urge to stand on his own feet. By sheer hard work he rose to become a flourishing barrister, which enabled him to lead a life of comfort and luxury, and adopt a western lifestyle. But his contact with Mahatma Gandhi transformed him, and he soon adopted the Gandhian way of life.

He was a multi-faceted personality in modern political Indian history. As an administrator he had no equal. He was the unifier of India, as we understand it today. He was a front ranking administrative actionist. He accomplished his mission of unifying India in less than five years.

Sardar Patel was a rare combination of a statesman and an administrator. A statesman has a vision, a perspective, a framework, but he need not be a good administrator, he may not know how to get his vision realized. Similarly, an administrator may not have a dream, a vision. Sardar Patel was both a far-sighted statesman and an able administrator.

In 1918 when there was a flood in Kaira, the British insisted on collecting tax from the farmers. This time the Sardar made optimum use of *Satyagraha* and asked the farmers not to give in to the demands of the government. All of this was done peacefully and the farmers followed his guidance. The British got fed up and eventually returned the land confiscated by them earlier.

In 1928 the farmers faced a similar problem and Vallabhbhai came to their rescue again. The British were as usual demanding an unjust tax and the farmers of Bardoli under the supervision of Vallabhbhai did not budge. The government in retaliation seized the lands. This agitation took on for more than six months until Patel's brother, Vithalbhai, an important figure in the Central Legislative Assembly struck a truce. This event immensely delighted Gandhiji and the title of 'Sardar' was conferred on him. When he was assisting Gandhiji in the Salt *Satyagraha*, he faced imprisonment for the first time As [the] president of the Indian National Congress, in 1931, Sardar Patel criticized public administration for its extravagance. He said:

"It would be too great a strain upon our poor purse to have to pay by way of insurance against corruption a premium out of all proportion to the highest possible estimate of corruption that may even take place."

He concluded:

"It will therefore, be necessary if India is to come to her own, to demand a heavy reduction in the Civil Service expenditure and a consequent reduction in the emoluments of the civil service."

He exercised the utmost care in looking after the financial accounts of the Congress during his tenure as its president. He kept an eye on the party machine as well as the Congress ministries. He would not spare anyone found indulging in corruption. He openly expressed his displeasure when one R. K. Sidhva of Sindh did not deposit to the party the funds collected for the Karachi Congress Session in 1931, and even ***"threatened to take disciplinary action if the amount was not refunded"***.

It is futile to look over Sardar Patel as an administrative Pluto immersed in propounding an administrative Utopia. Patel was earthy, and also down to earth. He was a realist, and was imbued with a single unwavering goal. He was a staunch patriot and his sole mission after achieving independence was to achieve unification of India and to strengthen its public administration, the prime instrument of both stability and development. His realism gave him flexibility of approach.

In the interim government formed in 1945 Sardar Patel became the Home Minister. In addition, he was the minister for information and broadcasting as well as for princely states. In India, the Home department has always been the most sensitive one, easily towering over the others, more so during those tumultuous days. Sardar Patel was in charge of home and as such bore the direct responsibility of steering the newly born republic through the extremely troubled times of the early period. As the portfolio of Civil Service fell within the charge of the Home department, Patel got the welcome opportunity of designing a civil service to answer the call of national unity, democracy and development.

And in the resolution of administrative problems, he rallied round career civil servants, even treating them as trusted advisors and administrators. Patel was a severe critic of the ICS before independence but emerged as its champion and advocate once freedom was won. In independent India, he needed the members of the ICS - perhaps as much as they [the members of ICS] needed him. Sardar Patel had been a critic of the colonial bureaucracy in India. But with independence in sight, he became a staunch supporter of the same organization, and wanted it to be strengthened in independent India. Patel regarded the 'steel-frame' as the bulwark of independent India's administrative unity and was convinced that administrative unity, which was vital for independent India, could only be secured by the retention of the steel-frame. On hearing about the Secretary of State's discontinuance of recruitment to the ICS, Patel acted swiftly and, within two days, convened what is known as the Provincial Premiers Conference to consider the alternative arrangements necessary. The Times [London] thus commented on the Secretary of State's decision to terminate recruitment:

"The sooner the Secretary of State's Control is ended and the present structure wound up, the better."

The interim government under the Prime Ministership of Jawaharlal Nehru was installed in 1946, with independence well in sight now. When a New India was in the offing the institution of all-India services, at one time the proverbial thorn in the Indian leadership's flesh, began to be wooed; and in this saga Sardar Patel played a pioneering role.

With the plan of resurrection of "All India Administrative Service" in his mind, Sardar Patel Convened a Conference of Provincial Premiers on 20th and 21st of October 1946. These who were invited to the conference were the provincial premiers but the provinces ruled by non-congress parties were represented either by a politician of minister's rank or civil servants. Its revenue minister represented Punjab, where the unionist party was in power. Sindh deputed its Chief Secretary whereas Bengal, where the Muslim League was in power, sent a civil servant of the rank of additional secretary.

Sardar Patel expressed the central government's support for the setting up of an All India Administrative Service; and the advantages he cited were many and were to both the Centre and the provinces. Such an All India Service would facilitate liaison between the Centre and the provinces, ensure certain uniformity in the standards of administration, and keep the central administration in touch with ground level reality. He went on to emphasize that the provincial administration would on its part acquire a wider outlook and obtain the best material for higher posts. He emphasized that there was [a] need for ensuring contentment and security in the services and that it was free from communal or party bias.

Sardar Patel, the "Iron man of India", emphasized on the formation of an Indian Administrative Service and with his strong will power he succeeded to do so. Accepting the suggestion of Govind Ballabh Pant, he recommended a combined Competitive Examination for the proposed Administrative Service and the Indian

Foreign Service. The central government would determine its own requirements, and after receiving the provincial proposals would work out the details of the cadre.

Sardar Patel also supported the creation of the Indian Administrative Service and the Indian Police Service. He wanted these services, and he got them. All this was a magnificent victory for the culture, and more truly, a personal triumph for Sardar Patel for which he worked as a great administrator. Indeed, Patel may, rightly be acknowledged as the Father of All India Service.

Soon after independence, he invited a group of senior civil servants on his residence and talked to them. He had worked for years with ***"only one burning desire - to save the country"***. Patel invited them ***"to dedicate themselves equally to the service of the country"***. He did not promise them ***"in return anything more than the joy [and satisfaction] which he himself and colleagues had experienced through such single minded devotion to what they regarded as the supreme duties and which he was certain they too would experience"***.

In his own words:

"The Congress has not demanded over for the sake of power but for the sake of service. If you have narrow ideas like Sikhistan., Jatistan and Raja-sthan, I should like to say that the wor1d today is different. We cannot think of any such narrow ideology. Government must be that of the people - rich, poor, Hindu, Muslim, Parasee and Christian. We have to conduct governmental affairs in a manner that each one feels it is his own government. Times are such that government is of those who exert and not of those who sit idle. You should be certain how and for what purpose you use power. We have to utilize power for the welfare of the downtrodden."

Patel as an administrator wished for full freedom of the civil service to think and advise independently. It was only then that the political leadership could get the best out of the career bureaucracy. He categorically declared:

"My secretary can write a note opposed to my views. I have given that freedom to all my secretaries." "I have told them", he continued, ***"If you do not give your honest opinion for the fear that it will displease your minister, then, please you had better go. I will bring another secretary. I will never be displeased over a frank expression of opinion!"***

There is a story of a secretary from whom Patel sought advice and who before giving his opinion wanted to know if he wanted honest advice. He retorted:

"Does government pay you huge amount of money per month for your dishonest opinions? It is your duty to give an honest opinion, and it is for me to accept it or not."

Sardar Patel was not an administrative philosopher. He was an administrator, a realist solidly rooted in the soil, an actionist at that. He was a consolidator. Patel was empirical to his core. He had a flare for organization right since his early days. He has been described as ***"a natural administrator who did not seem to need experience."*** He was a great listener, and listened patiently to all sides of a case before taking a decision. He had the capacity to say 'No' to requests he felt were unacceptable [and had the power to challenge any action that could question national integration. In one of his speeches, regarding the problem of princely states, he said:

"I assure you that we are not going to let the grass grow under our feet. Even if all these troubles come at the same time, we have got resources which would enable use to stand up to all of them at the

same time. If they are anxious to challenge us, we would be ready to accept it. Let no state have evil designs on us or dream of extending its hegemony. Let them not entertain the fond hope of any Jatistan or Raja-sthan or Sikhistan. If they persist, all these dreamers will soon be disillusioned."

Besides being a great administrator he was a firm believer in discipline in life. Addressing to the students and teachers of the University of Allahabad he said that discipline is the very essence of the life. Without it anarchy and chaos are only the matter of time. It is as essential in our classrooms and on your playing fields as in your future. The country needs a trained and disciplined youth and not a rabble of irresponsible hot heads. Similarly you must have a vision and idealism. Unless you have a proud vision of the future of your motherland and an idealistic conception of her greatness and destiny, you can hardly realize the true measure of your present duties and responsibilities. But you must appreciate that in order to be able to do something in your life you must always have your feet firmly on the ground. Mere vision and idealism can lead you nowhere. You must translate these into hard facts and achieve your objectives in the grim field of realities. You must remember that it is the height of tragedy to have once high ambitions self-defeated. Instead, you must be made of the stuff that challenges pre-destined fate and mocks at adversities.

The approach of Sardar Patel was very pragmatic to the economic affairs of the country. But it was imbued with humanism and urgency of the time. More Production and Equitable distribution were the sheet anchor of his economic policy and with affair deal to all instruments of production, Sardar with his robust enthusiasm and prodigious zeal applied himself wholeheartedly to the work of economic reconstruction of the land with the same doggedness and spirit as he had applied himself in solving the problems of states. Soon after independence when the economic policies of India were taking a shape, Sardar Patel was wielding his mighty influence in welding Labour, Capital and Government to ensure plentiful production in the shortest time possible to provide relief and succour to the common man and make him feel the glow of *Swaraj*. After the independence, poverty was deep rooted in the society and there was a clamour for more wages but not for more production. The intentions were obvious. So Sardar Patel in his characteristic way of tackling men and matters left no stone unturned in veering Labour and Capital towards the goal of optimum production under the circumstances then prevailing. Be it noted that among the champions of Labour of his time, Sardar by virtue of his service to them from the latter half of twenties, was among the veteran in the line. But he wanted to reorient labour on truly nationalistic lines to mightily contribute to nation's welfare and progress and to assume his worthy role shaping the bright future for India.

Once addressing in Bombay he asserted that the future of India depends on whether we step up production of food, cloth, cement, iron and steel and other essential articles both for civil population and defence needs. This is necessary not only for banishing hunger and disease, but also for consolidating freedom that we have won after years of struggle. Today, labour is on the crossroad. If they take the right road and contribute their energies for strengthening the country, India will have a glorious future. But, if they are misled, and take the wrong path, they will go down in the ditch and it will lead every one of labourers and others to ruin and destruction. Sardar Patel may be called as one of the founding fathers of Indian National Trade Union Congress for, to him, essentially goes the credit of uniting under its banner various labour organizations of the country as were espousing the cause of labour on truly nationalistic lines. Industrial peace was the call of the time and Sardar Patel was much alarmed by the growing anti Indian trends in the labour ranks thanks to the utter exploitation of the trade union forum by communists, and, to a degree by the socialists of the day too. It was to check this sabotaging tide and to refashion Indian Labour Movement on constructive line to serve the best interest of India that Sardar played a decisive and timely part in erecting the country wise fabric of Indian National Trade Union Congress

I can say that Sardar Patel is like an institution from which we the younger generation can learn a lot. Believing in oneself and working with complete honesty and discipline in one's life is essential for one's growth and progress to the sky. This is the lesson that we all can learn from the worthy life of Sardar Patel. If we as youth of India can imbibe some of his great qualities it would be a heartily tribute to ***The Iron Man of India***.

22

SARDAR PATEL: AN EXTRAORDINARY STATESMAN OF THE WORLD

Karin Preisendanz

On the death of Sardar Patel, leaders from all over the world sent their condolences. This was quite natural. Sardar Patel was such a great statesman of the 20th century who not only built a new India but also left a mark of his thoughts on international affairs.

The task that Sardar Patel accomplished of the unification of India will remain an everlasting part of the contemporary history of India. The Indians may not forget his noble works for thousands of years. Although the work completed by him for national integration is such that it can be the subject of several volumes and a similar example cannot be found in a thousand years of the history of the India. But in nutshell, the main reason behind the completion of this noble work of integration of India was his mature thinking. He developed his thoughts on the basis of the contemporary social and political conditions of India.

Sardar Patel knew that for long India had been under the foreign rule; the society had been suffering through evil traditions and economic backwardness. He well understood the impulse of mind of the common people of India. Therefore, on deciding on a solution to a problem, Sardar Patel took quick action. He always disliked a delay in the action. This policy of him remained successful. On the basis of this, he was successfully able to solve all the problems that emerged during the process of the integration of India. Not only had this but he also upheld the same policy in solving all other problems that emerged during and after independence of India.

When we discuss the policy upheld by Sardar Patel in solving a problem, we should note that it consisted of minimum use of power. Although Sardar Patel resolved most of the problems on the basis of harmony but in some cases he also took recourse of diplomacy. He was at perfection in raising his viewpoint and remained successful in it. It was on the basis of his above policy that he was able to serve the nation and play a decisive role in the building of a new India. As the British Prime Minister C. R. Attlee also admitted:

"Sardar Patel played an outstanding part in the great events of his generation and his name will have a permanent place in the annals of India."

After the two World Wars started a new era of international politics and equations. The U. S. S. R. and the U. S. A. stood opposite to each other. An era cold war started between them. The world was divided into two groups. Most of the countries of the world came either close to U. S. S. R. or the U. S. A. Rest of the countries and unions were also affected by the new developments. In such a situation, Sardar Patel understood the reality. He very rightly analysed the policy of gains of the U. S. S. R. and U. S. A. and called upon India to be cautious.

Sardar Patel advised to establish relations with other countries keeping the national interest supreme in the new international equations. Not only had this but he also called upon the other nations of the world to go ahead in accordance with this policy. This was an astounding thing. He laid emphasis on establishing relations of his country with Israel, Korea and U. S. A. and cautioned on establishing relations with China. This was the result of his foresightedness and also of his ability to understand the situation minutely. Sardar Patel was a supporter of the ideals of the U. N. O. That's why on the death of Patel the President of the General Assembly of the United Nation, Nasrollah Entezam, said:

"The world has lost a great man who staunchly supported the ideals of the United Nations..."

Sardar Patel believed that U. N. O. could prove to be a most successful organization in resolving world problems, eradicate worldwide injustice and in assuring freedom and equality to everyone. And this should be done. But for this purpose, it would be necessary that the U. N. O. is free from the claws of evil and selfish international politics. All member nations should have a constructive role in the U. N. O. and its programs should have active support from people of the world. Sardar Patel suggested the working of the U. N. O. to be based on mature and effective views. There is no doubt that Sardar Patel was a great and respected statesman. His works and thoughts are a legacy not only for his countrymen, but also for the people of the rest of the world.

23

SARDAR VALLABHBHAI PATEL AND EDUCATION: A PERSPECTIVE

Ravindra Kumar

Sardar Vallabhbhai Patel was a born leader who had a strong will-power, determination, unselfishness and the feeling of social-service. He was a self-made man. He had to face all sorts of problems of family, of society and of the nation, and had to carve out of a future for himself. It is for his qualities of head and heart, determination, a close perception of problems, rational thinking, and timely judicious actions that he will ever be remembered in the history of India. It will not be an exaggeration if we say that he was much greater than Bismarck for the unification of India.

Sardar Patel was a practical thinker. He opened his mind unhesitatingly on various important issues concerning the management of economy, nationalism, communal harmony and the international affairs. He was always right in his assessment of a situation, how much complicated it might be, and also in the solution he suggested whether accepted or not. Besides being a renowned statesman and a great administrator, he was an educationist also. Like Mahatma Gandhi, he had a clear concept of the system of education most suited to the people of independent India. He forthrightly expressed his views on this matter on several occasions. But, before we consider his views, it is necessary to analyze the then existing system of education.

India attained freedom in 1947. The education as imparted to the Indians was somewhat filtered education, the foundation of which was laid by Lord Macaulay who had little regard for Indian Culture and literature present or past. Moreover, it was introduced to achieve two objectives; one to prepare a class of bureaucrats from among Indians who had the appearance of the natives, but the mind and thinking of the British rulers and could help to rule over the country on behalf of the British Empire; the other to prepare a class of ***'babus'*** to work in offices. The medium of instruction was English, the syllabuses loaded with English language, literature, history, culture and the information incompatible with Indian thought and culture. Moreover, the education did not reach the masses and most of the populace remained illiterate.

Sardar Patel was a genius and was gifted with far-sightedness. He had a clear perception of the inconsistencies in the then existing system of education and realized that such a system would not be meaningful and effective to build up the independent India in Indian perspective. He was a staunch follower of Gandhian philosophy and fully agreed with his views on education. Gandhi regarded ethics and morality and basic [*buniyadi*] or technical education as the fundamental bases to make education meaningful.

Sardar Patel was born in a family of farmers and had a rural background. Since his childhood he had experienced the draw-backs of the then system of

There are many factors that are responsible for this sordid state of affairs, but the role of education, primarily the main factor, cannot be set aside. Education and culture are two aspects of civilization. Education cultivates a brute to become worthy and civilized. It is said:

"VIDYA DADATI VINAYAM,
VINAYAT YATI PATRATAM"

[Meaning thereby: Education makes a man humble, and with humility comes worthiness.]

The education that fails to inculcate ethical and moral values, cooperation, love, self-dependencies and many others can never be meaningful and is most likely to lead to disaster.

It is high time that the education-planners should sit together and evolve a system with emphasis on work-culture, ethical and moral values. It should be people-friendly and maintain a balance between academic and practical knowledge. Ours is an agricultural country. Even today most of its population lives in rural areas. Our economy also based on it to a great extent. Besides, the industrialization is also growing. Under these circumstances, a system based on the needs of the majority and which, co-ordinates the industries also will prove to be effective. Sardar Patel held these views and this sort of co-ordination in mind. It will bring a change in man and society. Inspired by Sardar Patel, the foundations of ***Charottar Vidya Mandal*** and the ***Charottar Gramodyog Sahakari Mandal***, in Gujarat have proved the test of time and have taken gigantic leaps. They are the living example of Sardar Patel's mature mind and rational thinking. I think that due to implementation of his ideas, while formulating education policies, will remove the draw-backs of the present day system of education, will make it more effective and help the people and the economy of the country.

24

SARDAR VALLABHBHAI PATEL: ARCHITECT OF INDIA'S UNITY

N.V. Gadgil

Three score and ten is the period allowed by the Prophet for a man to do his job in this world. Sardar Patel has already crossed this parallel and is marching ahead. It may be stated that the job he has before himself in a sense is still to be completed. Seventy-five years of life is not a small period, and yet there have been, and are, very few people in this country who have done or are doing a tenth of what Sardarji has done or is doing.

In 1948, while inaugurating one of the Unions[1] I stated that Gandhiji was the architect of our Freedom and Sardar was the architect of our Unity. Very few people realized how tremendous and how terrible the task of consolidation of freedom was in the initial period, following the dawn of Independence. There were not a few here, and abroad, who believed honestly that the Freedom of India would be a nine days' wonder in the hands of Indian leaders. Today there is none who dispute the great achievement of consolidation, and there is none who dispute the great and effective part Sardar has played in this process.

It was indeed a remarkable feat on the part of Sardar who had, and still has, the reputation as possessing a bitter tongue, that he should have, according to all people, adopted the policy of sweet reasonableness and constructive generosity in dealing with Princely India. The dividends earned by this policy are indeed great, and the aftermath of liquidation of feudal rule is not only bitter, but even the parties' concerned feel that they have got a square and honest deal. Indeed, there are persons who feel that the Princely Order has not yet been liquidated. It was one of the greatest principles of Gandhiji to make a distinction between the act and the actor and I should say the same has been a principle of great importance with Sardar. The Princes if distinguished from their rule are not all bad; some of them are equal in character and capacity with many of the leaders in this Democracy. What Sardar has done is something that leaves the person concerned with a feeling that his interest lies in approximating his life with the general trend of it in the community. If today some sum is guaranteed to certain Princes, it does not mean that those who receive it constitute a class or an order. It merely means that normal expectations should not be frustrated violently and the process of reconstruction of society, with a view of making it a classless one, must be of gradual and evolutional in spirit and character if enduring are to be attained.

People accuse Sardar of being a champion of the Capitalist System of Society. I do not share that view. It is no doubt true that his relations with the capitalist class are intimate and cordial. In this he is following in the footsteps of Mahatmaji. But at the bottom he has still the instinctive distrust about the rich that is so characteristic of a peasant. if today Sardar feels that things should move slowly, that social ownership and control should be gradual, the reason that he is very anxious for actual results. Like a shrewd peasant, as he undoubtedly is, basically, he considers one gain of practical achievement better than a ton of theories. Essentially he is pragmatic and "*a priori*" considerations have no validity for him. In this age of planning everything from birth to death, an outlook of this character may not find favour with the people at large. Undoubtedly most of us stand for a planned economy; for we feel that this policy of laissez-faire cannot go on creating an atmosphere all-around. A sense of equality and fulfilment is only possible in a planned economy. This could make us intolerant of any other point of view, in fact, it should be our concern to convince and convert other people to our point of view. I can speak from my personal experience that whatever may be Sardar's views on any subject, he is not dogmatic.

Sardar Saheb's contribution during the period preceding Independence is so great that it is not possible to think of India before 1947 without thinking of Sardar. From 1917 till 1947, over a period of 30 years, what Gandhiji conceived, Sardar concretised and carried out. It will be doing no injustice to Mahatmaji if it were to be stated that his *Satyagraha* became acceptable to political India only after the success of Bardoli peasants in their *Satyagraha* of 1928. The Bardoli struggle illustrated the Philosophy of *Satyagraha* in action and the efficient and effective leadership of Sardar was the main factor that achieved the result. That thousands of peasants should be ready to lose their all is a testimony to his determined leadership as well as to the unique faith the followers had in the leader. A great philosopher has said that the scars on the body disappear and are forgotten in life, but the scars on property are not only forgotten in life, but are carried over as inspiring mandates for generations to come. But in Bardoli, it was illustrated that there were at least some people who considered ideals as of greater value than material gain, who preferred principles to properties.

What was there in the leadership that brought about these results? What are the foundations of Vallabhbhai's leadership? A leader must inspire confidence and above all must inspire love and respect in his followers. People admire brilliance, respect character and adore love. Vallabhbhai loves his followers with the result that they follow him through thick and thin, irrespective of consequences. It is true that occasionally he is harsh. Very often he is considered unjust. But in all such cases, the measure is wrongly applied. In the ultimate analysis it will be found that his harshness and so-called unjust behaviour were in the interests of the cause that he and the person concerned espoused as their own. Although, unfamiliar with the theory and practice of military strategy, he has both by instinct and training a flair for fixing up the right moment to attack and the determination to see the action through. Success depends in choosing the right men, right material and the right moment and co-coordinating these three and driving them to the desired goal. In this context, it may be said that Vallabhbhai has shown that he understands the science of success and is immune from the feeling that represents failure as an art. Essentially, people love success, and normally they follow a successful leader. In politics and in war, achievement is an index of ability, though history has shown that many high personalities showed themselves to advantage in moments of defeat. Whatever it may be, the belief in this country is that to whatever field Sardar may direct his attention, success follows. There may be no rational explanations for this, but it is a fact that requires no emphasis.

The task before the country today is to complete the process of consolidation and to lay the foundations of prosperity. In the solution of this problem the statesmanship that is appropriate is one which takes due notice of what is today, what is possible tomorrow and what is desirable the day after that. In other words, vision, determination, a capacity to adjust the mind, a temper that will not lose its mornings-these are the elements that constitute such statesmanship. Sardar Vallabhbhai has this. Although he has a right to well-earned rest, yet the country demands his services for at least some time more. May he live long to see this country prosperous and progressing!

25

Reminiscence of Vallabhbhai

N.V. Gadgil

Why, Kaka! What are you doing? I replied that I was bathing in the Tungbhadra. This conversation took place in *Yeravada* jail in 1914. The person asking the question was a great worker and leader of the country. Individual *Satyagraha* began in November-December, 1940. On the night of December 2, 1940 I was arrested and immediately taken to Yeravada jail. A few days earlier Sardar Vallabhbhai Patel, Sri Bhulabhaiji, the General Secretary of Bombay, Sri Kher, President of the Bombay Legal Circle, Sri Mavalankar and other gentleman had been taken to *Yeravada*. These persons were lodged in a section of *Yeravada* called *Andheri* No. 1. I, along with the workers of Poona, were lodged in a section adjacent to it called Andheri No. 2. Between the two sections was a wall some 9 feet high. We could not see anyone and, if the jail orders were obeyed, we could neither talk to one another. This wall, as it were, had been raised between friends and between leaders. Those in No. 1 adhered to Gandhism very strictly and considered obeying prison rules a chief feature of Gandhism. Some workers like me were not prepared to allow such great importance to this prison rule, and, from the practical point of view too, we did not consider it proper that friends of leader and follower may not talk even when they are near or that they should be so restricted. There was no question of any principle in it. But Gandhiji had made the background of individual *Satyagraha* such that obeying prison rules was a condition of it. Just as there were some in No. 2 who would not obey this rule, there were some in No. 1 too which we called *Harijan Niwas*. However, at 9 one day I heard the above mentioned question from Vallabhbhai. At that time we, in our barrack, were taking bath. And the arrangement for bathing was this: There was something like a tank in the open field. Prisoners took cold water from it and had a bath. We had named it Tungbhadra, and, therefore, when I heard Sardarji's question, I gave the above mentioned reply. There were some other thing discussed too, but it was the first occasion when the inmates of *Harijan Niwas* tried to have a talk with persons residing with us. I know that Sardarji had wished for such unimportant conversation for many days and he took this step because he was an expert and loved his followers. It was an ordinary incident but it had great purpose and meaning.

I continued to experience this nature of Sardar Saheb more and more in the future. Sardar Saheb is leader who produces in the heart of his followers not only respect but devotion too.

If, in view of his features, one calls Sardar Saheb a man of strict nature it would not be wrong, but it is not his true personality. He is actually as soft as he seems to be hard. I have seen that about some incidents his cruelty and strictness was great but selfless, and I have seen such incidents too where his heart seemed to be soft as butter. Harder than thunder and softer than flowers, Vallabhbhai is super human. I have no doubt about it. I do not find the personality of any present

Indian so impressive and successful. How did he achieve his present position in the political field of India today and what is his specialty that we may consider the cause of his influential personality. Words and deeds show the personality of a man.

The correct method is to measure a man from the work he does. I think that among the present politicians it is only Sardar Saheb who speaks the least and works more than anyone else. It is not that when he speaks his words are charming. Neither has his statement a fold of figures of speech like simile and metaphor etc. But his statement certainly has irony, pun and suggestiveness and consequently it is very and for those who are the object of his words. Sardar Saheb is a child of a farmer family and we see it in its extreme the special nature of farmers in him. Just as a farmer separates grain and husk and understands well the true thing, Sardar Saheb too at once sees what is real, however intricate the problem and however difficult the times. And because he sees it clearly he can easily find out the proper solution for it.

The work is successful when the worker understands his object well and collects the material properly. This depends on all three-determination, material and time. If a man changes his determination every moment, his work will never attain success. Material can be of two kinds: one conserving man and the other conserving things. If these two are not properly adjusted, failure in the work is certain. Even when one has determination and material both, the aim cannot be achieved if time is not favourable. Therefore, great men first establish their aim, collect the material and make their efforts as soon as time is favourable and achieve fame. If we examine, from this point of view, what Sardar Saheb did, we come to the conclusion that Sardar Saheb has worked accordingly to all those principles.

If, I think, Sardar Saheb had not been there, the freedom of India should have remained fragmentary. Today, if all the States have disappeared and India is united, all the credit for it goes to Sardar Saheb alone. I do not think that our people have fully appreciated the work that Sardar Saheb did. When the picture is very near, its beauty or accomplishment cannot be fully appreciated. If we look at the same picture from some distance its grandeur beauty and art can be seen better. The same applies to the happening in life. After 15 or 20 years Indians will understand well and they will also acknowledge properly that the work Sardar Saheb did was epoch making and great.

The life-work of Vallabhbhai can be described in these two expressions; great work and world fame. When I see how he did not like fame, I am reminded of the expert politician of Maharashtra, Nana Phadanavis. About him a historian has written that when he spoke his words were precious like pearls and his work was so extensive for which there can be no smile. In spite of all this, his work was never boastfully proclaimed. The same historian says that the custom amongst Muslims was that the least of work was extolled as immense and annals of it were written, but Nana Phadanavis did not only consider his great work even small, but also did not talk of it. Such a view can be expressed about Sardarji too.

Today Sardar is completing 75 years of his journey of life. During the last 30 years his life and the life of the nation were not different. The famous saint of Maharashtra, Tuka Ram has said that charitable acts are still to be performed. This is Sardarji's life. One never felt that he had some personal life too. His life has fully become the life of the nation. As the Gita says, ***"Dedicate to God all that you do, all that you eat and whatever you speak".*** Similarly Sardar Saheb has offered the lotus of his life at the feet of *Bharat Mata*.

Appendix-A

[Suggestions at the Meeting of Representatives of the East Punjab States]

I need hardly dwell at any great length on the magnitude, urgency and supreme importance of the problem of speedy evacuation and resettlement of refugees. For the moment, the first question is uppermost in our minds and I shall therefore take it up in the first instance.

As all of you are probably aware, compulsion of events have necessitated evacuation of millions of men, women and children from West Punjab to East Punjab and from East Punjab to West Punjab. This evacuation naturally includes a large population who have their roots in the neighbouring States and in whom these States are bound to be as much interested as we are. *In a reciprocal measure of this kind, it is impossible for us to look upon matters purely from the point of view of communities in which we are interested.* We have, therefore, to ensure smooth and undisturbed passage not only of non-Muslims coming from West Punjab but also of Muslims going from this side.

It is of the utmost importance that this process of evacuation should get all possible help and facility by all the means at our disposal, and I should like to remind you that in this matter time is of the essence. If we cannot evacuate within as short a time as possible, we shall be faced with consequences too terrible to contemplate. It is, therefore, with great concern and anxiety that we have been observing recently the mounting toll of hold-ups of trains that has greatly hampered the progress of evacuation. Even, otherwise, our refugees on the other side were being attacked by the various elements of the West Punjab. Attacks on refugee trains lead to retaliations which are much more dangerous and savage. Besides these mad and furious attacks by unruly mobs on our normal lines of communications is a direct challenge to the authority of our State as well as yours and no Government worth the name can tolerate this for a moment. *It is, therefore, in the interests of our own refugees coming from West Punjab that we should take steps to ensure smooth and safe evacuation of those who want to go away from India.* Moreover, it having been decided that these Muslims have no place in areas where they were residing, or those who are willing or anxious to go, the sooner they leave India, the better in the interests of all concerned. This would save us from many problems, particularly of food and law and order; and, therefore, it is essential that we should send them away as quickly as possible.

As far as I have been able to visualize this problem of ensuring safe passage for these refugees, it is not only a question of escort for the trains but also of supplementary ground action. Such ground action must take two forms. One is ensuring the responsibility of the villagers residing in the neighbouring villages from whom the disturbing elements must be attracting some sympathy for the success of their operations. Such a collective responsibility involves the collection of intelligence and imparting of information to responsible authorities about the assembly of *jathas**, patrolling of

* A small group of people, gathering, an attacking party.

the tracks lying in particular areas, prompt reports of attacks and identity of attackers. *It is obvious that, if the villagers fail in these important matters, the only way punishment can devolve on them is by resort to imposition and recovery of collective fines.* But I must emphasize that for these fines to be effective, it is necessary that they should be imposed immediately and recovered promptly and the amounts must be substantial. More stringent measures, more or less similar to those taken during the war period, of compelling able-bodied villagers to take up the responsibility of personally guarding the lines should be taken. The other means of supplementing escorts would be by adequate ground action, particularly to comb out nests of these *jathas* and to cover up the tracks of these *jathas* once the y have been engaged by the escorts. To my mind, one of the reasons why these *jathas* have been acting with impunity is the almost complete absence of the visitation of punishment, apart from casualties inflicted by escorts. *It is clear that we must remedy this grave lacuna in our machinery to deal with this menace for without this we would be seriously crippling the action that we propose to take.*

It has occurred to me that the best way to tackle this problem would be to organize highly mobile patrols in these areas. It would be the business of these patrols to post themselves with information from villages, etc., regarding the assembly of these *jathas* and to exercise particular vigilance when a refugee train is passing through their jurisdiction. For this purpose, it is essential that both the patrols and the escorts of trains should be equipped with wireless sets. These patrols would also follow the trains by road that generally skirts along the railway line at some distance. In the first place, the attackers would find it difficult to assemble for attacks; secondly, even if they succeed in assembling, they would be caught between two fires and it would be impossible for them to escape the punishment of their crimes.

The third point should, in my opinion, be the effective organization of intelligence in the areas in which these *jathas* operate. For this purpose, *it is essential that the civil authorities co-operate and co-ordinate with the Military* and it will be necessary for us to establish contacts and sources in villages in the vicinity of railway lines. I myself feel that, if we could successfully accomplish these three methods of combating this very serious problem, we shall have ensured as perfect a safety for the refugee trains as possible and thereby we shall have facilitated the evacuation of millions of our men on the other side.

The second problem is that of rehabilitation of refugees. The matter is so sacred and the obligation so humanitarian that I do not think it is necessary for me to appeal for your sympathy and co-operation. I take these for granted. *We have millions to settle on lands or in business and occupation of one kind or another.* Many will probably settle down in the places vacated by the outgoing Muslim refugees. Many will need help and encouragement from us. They will need understanding and sympathy. *In this task, it is necessary that the States and the Province of East Punjab and the Central Government should all lend their hands without any motive of profit or selfish gain, but actuated entirely by a desire to assist in a humanitarian cause.* At the same time, I fully realise that there are limitations to absorptive capacity. Even then we should all stretch our resources to the maximum extent possible to accommodate them and I hope we can look forward to the co-operation of those present here in this great task.

Appendix-B

[The Preventive Detention Bill]

At the outset, I should like to apologize to the House for the extremely short notice at which I have to approach it for this emergency legislation. The legislative output of the Ministry to which I have the honour to belong has not been large. That, I hope, would be regarded as sufficient proof of my intention not to trouble the House or to trouble the House only when no other course is available to me. In this particular instance also, I plead the same urgent necessity.

The honourable members are aware that the old Constitution in certain respects died on 26 January midnight when the new Constitution was born and the order of the President in this respect was signed at ten o'clock on the next day. So there was an interregnum which the lawyers cannot excuse; and, therefore, to cover up this lacuna, it has become a necessity. Besides, certain judicial pronouncements or decisions during the last couple of weeks and certain litigation which is pending before the Courts have created a situation in which, I feel, having regard to the conditions prevailing today, that unless this House takes immediate action, a grave peril to the security of the State is involved. That, therefore, is my justification for approaching this House with this piece of legislation.

The House or at least the majority of the members of this House who were members of the Constituent Assembly are aware of the prolonged discussions which we had on Article 22 of the Constitution and the final form which that Article took. I can say straightway that unfortunately owing to my ill-health, I could not be present when the discussions were going on. But I was very apprehensive that certain aspects regarding the security of the State were not properly emphasized before the House, at that time; and, with all the respect to that august body, I felt that due weight was not given to those considerations. But I thought that the House also has provided for another alternative which, if resorted to, would meet with the requirements of the case and that under Section 373*, the President's help would give a breathing period. *Fresh legislation would, in any case, has been necessary because of the limitations placed by article 22nd the powers of the States to keep a person under detention.*

Recently the judgment of the Patna High Court declaring the Local Public Safety Act as *ultra vires* the Constitution on account of its having certain provisions inconsistent with the Constitution has created difficulties in that Province. The Calcutta High Court is already cognizant of an application made by 350 detenus who, I am assured, are some of the most dangerous persons. The Bombay High Court have also released some of the detenus the other day because they found that it was contrary to the provisions of the Constitution to keep them under detention any longer. The High Court of Allahabad has also issued an order declaring certain provisions of the Public Safety Act to be inconsistent with the provisions of the Constitution. These judicial pronouncements have, therefore, created a situation in more than one Province in which it would no longer be

* Of the Constitution of India.

possible for us to keep under detention persons about whose dangerous and subversive activities the State Governments have no doubt.

Here, I should like to remind the House that the State Governments at our instance have already introduced in their Public Safety Ordinances or legislation machinery some type of Advisory Boards as referred to in article 2 of the Constitution which scrutinizes cases of detention and makes suitable recommendations. In a large majority of cases of those who are at present under detention, the Government has had the concurrence of these advisory bodies. It is only in comparatively small number of cases that these Governments have had to invoke the primary responsibility which they have of maintaining law and order and to keep the persons under detention even if the Advisory Boards felt otherwise. The House, therefore, can rest assured that a large majority of the cases with which it is dealing at present had the scrutiny of a non-executive authority.

I shall not weary the House by telling it how exactly the Communists in India who have been by far the largest number of detenus constitute a danger to the existence and security of the State which has been brought into being by the sacrifices and sufferings of the millions of our people. It would be a poor return for those sacrifices and sufferings if we fail to preserve the liberties which we have won after so much struggle and surrender them to the merciless and ruthless tactics of a comparatively small number or persons whose inspiration, methods and culture are all of a foreign stamp and who are, as the history of so many countries shows, linked financially, strategically, structurally and tactfully with foreign organizations.

If anybody wishes to seek justification for our policy against them in cold print he can do so in the pages of the pamphlet which we issued last year illustrating the methods and instances of Communist violence. *I should like to say here that our fight is not with Communism or with those who believe in the theory of Communism, but with those whose avowed object it is to create disruption, dislocation and tampering with communications, to suborn loyalty and make it impossible for normal government based on law to function.*

Obviously, we cannot deal with these people in terms of ordinary law. Obedience to law should be the fundamental duty of a citizen. When the law is flouted and offences are committed, ordinarily, there is the criminal law which is put into force. But where the very basis of law is sought to be undermined and attempts are made to create a state of affairs in which, to borrow the words of the distinguished patriot*, the father of our Prime Minister, when "men would not be men and law would not be law", we feel justified in invoking emergent and extraordinary laws.

Sir, there are also other anti-social elements raising their heads and troubles of very serious dimensions are well above the horizon. I know honourable members are already concerned about some of the recent developments. I am sure the House would like us to be fully armed and equipped with the means of dealing with any emergency that might arise. There is, therefore, a full justification for the enactment of a special measure to deal with persons of the type we propose to cover by this Bill.

I shall now deal with the structure of the Bill. Under Article 22 of the Constitution, there are two sets of provisions relating to preventive detention. One set of provisions authorizes the detention of any person for a longer period that three months if an Advisory Board has certified that, in its opinion, there was sufficient cause for such detention. The other set of provisions

* Pt. Motilal Nehru, an eminent lawyer and a stalwart nationalist leader of the thirties

authorizes Parliament to make a law under which a person may be detained for a longer period than three months without obtaining the opinion of the Advisory Board and which also lays down the maximum period for which any person may, in any class of cases, be detained. As the provisions of the Bill will indicate, we propose to cover both these types of cases in this Bill. We have prescribed that for certain categories of detenus, namely, those detained in connection with the maintenance of supplies and services essential to the community, or who are foreigners, or who are detained by the District Magistrate or Sub-divisional Magistrate, or in a Presidency town, the Commissioner of Police, the Advisory Board would be the final authority to determine the question of the continued detention. In regard to the other categories of cases, that is, those who are concerned with the Defence of India, relations of India with foreign powers or the security of the State or the maintenance of public order, it will not be necessary to obtain the opinion of the Advisory Board. Nevertheless, we feel that some sort of a non-executive authority should be associated with the Government in a purely advisory capacity even in regard to these cases. We have, therefore, provided that after a period of six months of the original detention, the Government concerned shall review its decision in consultation with a judicial authority.

We have thus maintained not only the provisions of the Constitution, but also its spirit. What is more, we have gone a step further than the provisions of the Constitution in that even where it has armed the Parliament with powers to provide for detention without obtaining the opinion of an advisory board, we have sought to replace the Advisory Board by a judicial authority whose opinion though not as binding as that of the Advisory Board, will, still be entitled to weight and consideration.

The other provisions of the Bill are merely incidental and embody the procedural matters either in the existing Public Safety Legislation in the States or in the Constitution itself. We have provided, for instance, for communication to detenus the grounds on which the order has been made and affording them the earliest opportunity of making a representation against the order. We have also sought to preserve the secrecy of the information on which the detention order is based without in any way prejudicing an accused from seeking his own protection under the law. *Also in order to give this or the successor Parliament an opportunity to review matters after sometime, we have limited the life of the Bill up to 31st March 1951.*

Sir, I hope, I have now given sufficient justification of the urgency and necessity of this measure and have also shown conclusively how in framing its provisions we have safeguarded the liberty of the individual against the arbitrary acts of the executive.

I shall now only plead with the House that during the consideration of this measure it fully takes into account the dangers which happily we have so far avoided, the dangers which unhappily still threaten us and the explosive possibilities of the situation with which we are faced at present. *When we think of civil liberties of the extremely small number of persons concerned, let the House also think of the liberties of the millions of people threatened by the activities of individuals whose civil liberties we have curtailed. I am using the words "civil liberties" in connection with these individuals with some reluctance, because, for them liberty is synonymous with licence and there is hardly any difference between civil and criminal.*

APPENDIX-C

[SPEECH AT RED FORT, DELHI DATED 29 JANUARY 1950]

This exhibition was to be opened on January 26, the day we became a sovereign democratic republic. It shows the things manufactured in our country, in the villages and in the towns, handicrafts as well as machine-made products. We have to consider in which of these items we should expand production and which we should use more in the national interest.

Twenty years ago, in 1930, we pledged to work for complete independence. By God's grace we have redeemed that pledge; we need not go into the many causes due to which we did not have to suffer as much for it as we might well have suffered. But usually we do not value fully those things for which we do not have to suffer much. Gandhiji underwent the biggest suffering for *Swarajya*. There were others, too who followed in his footsteps and sacrificed a lot. It was no easy task to integrate such a big country, with its many religions and languages, which had never been one country. So many different States had to be integrated and organized in order that the whole country should be free. But we had comparatively little trouble; we have, therefore, not enough appreciation for this. That however is not the end of our task.

What has been achieved so far is like a peasant preparing the ground for cultivation. The true *Swarajya* of Gandhiji's dreams has still to be created by us in India. Those who held up our work have left. There is no obstacle now. But millions in our country are suffering today. They need food, clothing and shelter. At least there should be no lack of these things under self-rule. We do not grow as much food as we need. Burma (which was the source of a good deal of rice consumed in Madras and Bengal) and some of the food surplus areas in our country have now separated from us. There is thus a deficit. To ensure that food is available everywhere and no one starves, we have to import food grains. Arrangements have to be made to ensure at least subsistence rations everywhere, thus necessitating various controls. These lead to many evils. In such a big country, it is not easy to have rationing and controls. The Government is often brought into disrepute. People take bribes. Much else happens. But it is all our doing. Aliens have no hand in this. People blame the Government. To a certain extent they are right. But it also gives our people a bad name in the world – as people who cannot help each other at such a juncture, who cannot co-operate, cannot share. This is not good for us. It is not Gandhiji's way. If we want true *Swarajya*, we have to follow his way.

This exhibition shows, among other things, how to grow more food, what to do and use for this purpose, what we are doing in this respect and where. We have to become independent of food imports and mostly grow what we need. It is a difficult task, especially for a country weakened by years of slavery and foreign exploitation. A poor country does not become affluent only by achieving freedom. But if all work unitedly, it can be done.

Gandhiji said our *Swarajya* depended upon the *Charkha*; we could spin our way to Swarajya. But we did not do that. The *Swarajya* we have gained is not the real thing. Real *Swarajya* we can have by producing in our country what we need. For this we will have to change our habits. We will have to transform our villages. We have to pledge ourselves not to use imported goods. Of course, if there is anything not produced in our country, but required in the national interest to produce more wealth, like machinery, it will have to be used. But we should, as for as possible, not even touch foreign products. Things made by our poor brothers and sisters in our villages and our towns have to be encouraged. All free countries do this. Their people are taught this from childhood.

Our industrialists and other capable people should try to manufacture the machines we now import and make our economy self-reliant.

Unfortunately, we have a dispute with a neighbour of ours. We have the factories in Calcutta which used to utilize all the jute grown in Pakistan. The Government of India has done its best to see that economies of both the countries are not hampered. But no agreement that we reach is implemented by them. We have to act alone. They refuse to deliver even the jute paid for in advance, thus harming both countries. If they cannot guarantee to implement agreements, we had better not depend on them. Let us grow the jute and the cotton and the food grains we need. It is rather hard because we import a lot of food grains while they have enough and to spare; they got all the best cultivable and irrigated lands and turned out the occupants who are now refugees here. We have to make arrangements for these people bear with their anger and their sorrow, while their golden land has been usurped by others. We have asked loudly and repeatedly for a settlement but Pakistan obstinately refuses to do so. Thus the dispute lingers on. It can be resolved only by frank and broad-hearted fraternal talks.

It should be our effort to see that both we and our neighbour should prosper. But as long as our neighbour does not take kindly to our prosperity or delights in our discomfiture, we have to keep our distance from such a neighbour and make all arrangements for our security.

An exhibition of the kind organized here enables us to know what goods our country produces, to select the ones we need and like, and to prefer them to cheaper imported goods. If we will put up with some discomfort in this matter, for a year or three years or five years, our country will grow stronger and we will stand in fear of none. Today we have some kind of peace in the country, and it is united as never before. This is a big thing. But now our task is to keep it united. For this it has to be made strong by the common effort of us all. It cannot be done by depending on the government alone to do it. It has not the necessary resources. It is everyone's duty for the next three or four years to help the government in every way in strengthening the country by avoiding quarrels and controversy and engaging in constructive activities as depicted in this exhibition. The world today is full of conflict and strife. We should endeavour to save our country from getting involved in this. It is a difficult task but it is always exhilarating to work against heavy odds. Only cowards fear adversity.

Appendix-D

Convocation Addresses of Sardar Vallabhbhai Patel at the University of Nagpur, the Banaras Hindu University, Varanasi and the Allahabad University, Allahabad Dated 03-11-1948, 25-11-1948 and 27-11-1948 Respectively]

I must thank you for the affectionate and warm welcome which you have extended to me and for the love and regard which you have shown me by conferring this single honour on me. Gifts are of many kinds; those achieved by one's own endeavour are good and deserved, but no gift should be conferred on one whose worthiness has not been tested. By selecting me without assuring yourself of my fitness for the gift, you have laid me under a heavy debt; and, by your injunctions that I should continue to prove worthy of it throughout my life, you have imposed on me a very difficult obligation. At present, I cannot say anything because I am bound by your love and affection; and, therefore, with your blessings and God's grace, I pray that I may prove worthy of it. Should

I fail the blame for my failure will be shared by you as well.

On this occasion, I well remember of what I told you when I came here last.[1] Today also, ever since I have set my foot in Nagpur, the whole picture of Freedom Struggle is recurring to my mind with which Nagpur is so intimately associated. I recall the Annual Session of the Congress which laid found foundations of India's Independence.[2] I think of the meeting of the Working Committee of the A. I. C. C.[3] at Dhantoli, the arrest of the late lamented Shri Jamnalal Bajaj[4] and the Flag *Satyagraha* that followed.

On this occasion, I wish to place before you a few thoughts which occur to my mind as incidental to our hard-won our freedom. But just as I am doubtful if I deserved the honour that you have done me, you have also to think whether you have done everything to deserve the freedom that you have attained after such a bitter and sustained struggle.

There are people who think that having won freedom, there is nothing more to do about it. *Freedom has come to us through sacrifices.* Those who made sacrifices tasted the fruit of their efforts and self-denials, but it is for those who are now enjoying freedom to taste its fruit. After the last world war, there is an all-round deterioration in human standards. People have become self-centred. They have forgotten or ignored the wider interests of the country. *The essential and noteworthy features of our Struggle were: Sacrifice, Self-denial, Truth and Non-violence.* The weapons of the world war were: Violence, Brute Force, Political and Military moves and counter-moves. As a result of the churning of the ocean, the world has emitted poison. That poison is spreading all over and there is none to swallow it. The countries which were free have managed to digest it somewhat, but we who have just attained our Freedom are finding it hard to do the same. Therefore, those who think that having attained Freedom they have attained everything have really attained nothing! The Freedom that we have won is yet to be consolidated. *The foundations of Freedom have to be well and truly laid!* This one-year old child has to be nursed and nourished, instructed and strengthened. It is for us to do it and we must do it.

In India, today, there is no time for useless controversies and un-necessary debates and disputes. One can indulge in these pastimes when one has time and leisure. At present, we have to occupy ourselves with the all-absorbing task of making the foundations of our Freedom strong and unassailable. We have to reflect on our place in this broken and destructed world and what our duty and obligations are! If we will fail to make the best use of our Freedom to make it worthwhile and turn it to our advantage and advancement, future generations will heap curses on us. *They will say that a spiritualist, a great soul gave us this precious boon, but we did not know how to retain it and lost it.*

I would like to urge upon those who train citizens of the tomorrow and to those citizens of the morrow that we have yet to stand on our feet. *We must concentrate on one thing alone; viz., how to make our country strong and united.* We can make it strong when hearts are pure and when we fully appreciate our duty. Now that foreign rulers have gone, are we in a position to sustain the whole burden that has devolved on us? When we took over from them, the administrative fabric was in tatters. We have to mend and replace it. This, in itself, is a heavy responsibility. It is for our Universities to train young men to shoulder these responsibilities.

The great university of life is full of experiences, but to make full use of those experiences - all of us, students, teachers and professors - have to be cautious and on guard.

The most essential requisite is character. If your character is lacking and you leave the precincts of the *Alma Mater* without your character fully developed, you will be wasting an opportunity of a lifetime.

You have to realize that India has to attain its rightful place in the comity of Nations. The leadership of Asia would be hers if she conducts herself well and if her citizens make their fitting contribution to nation's resurgence. Whatever trials and troubles we might have passed through, it is no denying the fact that we have a precious inheritance and the teachings we have received from the departed leader are great assets for us.

India abounds in the resources of Nature and manpower. They are awaiting full use. That task must devolve on young men. We ourselves were trained in the school of experience. We fought for Freedom and we have attained that prize for you. It is now up to you to prove yourself worthy of the same. This you can do only if you work with single-minded devotion to the same of the country. It is only then that you can deserve this Freedom and be proud of it.

The real danger to India lies in our disunity. What poison of communalism was spread in the past? You should draw a curtain over it. Only then could we equip ourselves for the Freedom that has come to us. *There are still persons in the country whose loyalty to India has not settled down.* They should and will leave India.

Although our Freedom is hardly a year-old, we are thinking in terms of Maharashtrians, Gujaratis, etc. It is poisonous growth. You must avoid it. It is only the foolish and the ignorant who think on those lines. *Hyderabad was like an ulcer which has been operated upon.* The puss from that ulcer will persist for sometime. You have carefully to wash it off to see it disappear completely. You cannot assess the nature of that problem. History will assess it. You must only realize that we have many more ulcers of this kind still to be dealt with.

There were 562 States, - all separate units. When alien rulers left us we could settle that problem smoothly and without bloodshed. *In this very place I settled the problem of Chhatisgadh States.*[5] *In 12 hours, I had the authority of rulers in my pockets.* All this happened by mutual consultations and goodwill. There was no heart-burning, no discontent and no compulsion. We have to vouchsafe that the changes that we have wrought in the States are real changes and not mere changes of the map.

This is the occasion for mutual help and mutual cooperation. We must know what our duty is as true citizens. Your teacher has to impart that duty, I have heard of some Universities where some teachers believe in communalism and sectarianism. If we cling to these parochial ideas and exclude the larger aspect of the country, we shall not be strong. On the other hand, we shall be pulling down the structure of Freedom that we have built with so much of effort and sacrifices. Unless we learn to shoulder our responsibility in the true spirit of discipline and citizenship we cannot go ahead. We must strengthen our shoulders and our legs so that we can stand erect and bear the burden that has devolved on us. Then alone would we secure the real objective of Freedom.

I am grateful to you for your gift, but you know I am a farmer. As a farmer it is not my calling to receive gifts. I make no claims to learning. I have no degrees to be proud of, nor have I earned any. Nevertheless, in all humility, I accept what you have bestowed on me and pray that I might prove worthy of the same.

I agree with your Vice-Chancellor that here came[6] one and the sole leader of our Independence Movement, viz., Gandhiji. It was his austerity and his *tapasya*[7] that brought us this gift of freedom. I claim to be nothing more than an obedient soldier of him like the millions who obeyed his call. *There was a time when every one used to call me his blind follower, but both I and he knew that I followed him because our convictions tallied.* I am not one given to debates and verbal disputes. I have prolonged discussions. *For several years, Gandhiji and I were in perfect agreement. Mostly, we agreed instinctively; but when the time for a big decision on the question of India's Independence came we differed.* I felt that we had to take Independence there and then. We had, therefore, to agree to Partition. I came to this conclusion after a great deal of heart-searching and with a great deal of sorrow. But I felt that if we did not accept Partition, India would be split into many bits and completely ruined. My experience of office of one year[8] had convinced me that the way we were preceding we were heading for disaster. *Gandhiji felt that he could not agree with this conclusion. But he told me that if my heart bore testimony to the rightness of my convictions, I could go ahead.* Our leader whom he nominated as his heir and successor[9] was with me. Gandhiji did not oppose us nor did he consent to what we thought was right and proper. Even today I do not repent for having come to that decision, thought it was with a great wrench of the heart that we did so.

We undoubtedly made some mistakes. Its responsibility attaches to some people; but I do not wish to enter into those details. I am convinced that the decision we took was to the Nation's benefit. People do not know what would have happened if we had not accepted Partition. At the same time, we were convinced that partition was worth accepting only if the foreign power quitted as quickly as possible. We, therefore, made it a condition that we would accept the partition of the country if the British left in six or eight week's time. The pace at which the legislation[10] was passed and the unanimity behind it in the British Parliament were probably a record in British history.

It is for us to profit from our mistakes and not to persist in them. Our mistakes have made us feel ashamed before the world. Gandhiji's assassination was the direct consequence of those mistakes.

India today is one and united. There is no question now of any foreign pockets. As I came to the University, I saw placards and heard some shouts for the merger of Banaras State.[11] I fail to understand why people should worry about these small things. It is only a question of time. They way we settled the issue of Hyderabad must be an object-lesson to those who are indulging in this profitless endeavour.

The Maharaja of Banaras is one of us. We have only to make him understand the significance of the thing and I am sure he will not stand in the way. After we have secured Independence it is idle for us to think in terms of *Maharajas* or *Rajas*. They are all Indians. I never accepted that they were not patriots. They were under foreign domination as we were. Having become free, they have become one of us. Look at India's unity which we have today. All this has been achieved by following Gandhiji's methods. *Love and not conflict did the trick.*

But unity and integration are not enough. India has secured Freedom, but we show no signs of being a free people. I appeal to you, students and through you to all Indians, that we old men are now nearing the end of our journey. Whatever days are left for us, we shall devote them to your service and to the call of Nation. If you realize the true State of things, it is all right. Otherwise, there will be troublous times and great dangers. The whole of Asia is in turmoil. Can you escape from it? You can only do so if you would leave sectional loyalties aside and stand four squares behind the Nation's call and needs.

India's Freedom is only a year old. We have to nurse and nourish it. We have to devote proper care and attention for its growth. When India attains proper place in the comity of nations and has peace, tranquillity and contentment, you may have some leisure for your fancies. Today interests of the country call for heavier demands. It will be for you to shoulder the burden and responsibility of meeting these demands. We have secured Freedom for you. The way is open and clear. If you can do so, you may chalk out your own path to make India strong. If you can co-operate in this laudable and patriotic effort, you will do your duty.

It is not for you to involve in controversies. *Studies must claim your prior attention.* So long as you are engaged in studies, you have no time to waste in useless controversies. It behoves students to make the best use of their time and opportunities so that they may equip themselves for responsibilities that they would have to shoulder in their future careers. It is my firm view that it will not pay us in the long run to send so many students abroad for training or experience. On the other hand, we would do much better if we could concentrate on giving such training in India. If we have no professors of adequate qualifications we should rather have them here so that many might derive profit with a comparatively small expense. Otherwise, what is happening today? There are 300 to 400 scholars who are stranded abroad. We do not know how they would fare on their return! When it is admitted that the country should produce more, there are people who induce labourers to produce less and ask for more wages or go on strike. People think that whatever needs to be done must be done by

Government alone. This is a wrong approach to our problems as well as our duties. *The country expects every citizen to do his duty and not to wait for someone else to do it.*

This is undoubtedly the time when you must also develop your character. *Learning without character is a poor possession.* Gandhiji taught us how to make sacrifices. He taught us to be non-violent and disciplined. He also inculcated a feeling of brotherhood and comradeship. But today we are acting quite contrary to those teachings. Everyday we should think what we have done for our country and whether we have advanced its interests one way or the other.

If Pakistan goes its own way and becomes a theocratic State, ours is not that way. *While protecting our religion, we-have to follow the path whereby we can protect all creeds and religions.* Let us not get involved in communal wrangles. But, at the same time, we should guard ourselves against any danger to our national existence.

The very first thing that strikes a visitor to this University is its deep and intimate association with the late Pandit Madan Mohan Malaviya[12] of revered memory. He was a large-hearted man of broad vision. He planned the University with the same large-heartedness. All of you who are receiving instruction and inspiration from the Institution created by his vision and idealism should consider yourselves fortunate. I myself wish I enjoyed the same good fortune. After all, when you think of Malaviyaji and his association with this University, you cannot help asking yourselves if you are following his precepts and example. You have to ask yourselves how far you are contributing to the realization of his dreams. It is that question which must claim your attention so long as you are the alumni of this Institution.

I appeal to you to concentrate on the paramount need of the hour, namely, a constructive approach to the country's problem. Young men require training and practice in the art of defending themselves. We have to defend our country against any threat from outside. We are spending crores of rupees on Kashmir. We are spending lakhs on refugees. Our expenditure has increased beyond computation. Labour wants higher wages. Government servants also demand more. Where is all this money to come from? We have not enough to eat; so we have to import at tremendous cost. We spend crores on shipping and freight alone. It is obvious that if we have to exist we must produce more wealth; and, if we do not do so, we shall land ourselves in enormous difficulties and dangers.

This is the time for self-analysis and introspection for you. You have to think of the path that you should follow. Above all, it is your duty to maintain and enhance the prestige of your University. What amount of labour and what high purpose are enshrined in this Institution! You have to uphold them. You should not spend your time in mutual bickerings and quarrels. You should honour and respect your teachers and professors. Until you realize the utility of all this, you cannot prove worthy citizens of a free India and you shall not have appreciated the true worth of your Freedom. Just as I have to prove worthy of the honour which you have conferred on me, you also have to ensure that you bring nothing but credit to your Alma Mater. My prayers are with you!

References

1. For Nagpur University Convocation after the formation of Interim Government.
2. Sardar here refers to the Famous Session of the Congress at Nagpur during December 1920 when the Indian National Congress declared its goal of Swaraj by peaceful legitimate means. It was here that the Congress adopted almost wholeheartedly Gandhiji's programme of Non-co-operation.

3. Sardar here refers to the meeting of the Congress Working Committee and the A.I.C.C. in July 1923 which made an ignoble name because of open fight between the *Swarajists* and the Non- co-cooperationists.
4. As leader and organizer of the Nagpur Flag *Satyagraha* Shri Jamnalal Bajaj was arrested on 19 June 1923 and the Sardar had to lead this fight on till its successful culmination in September 1923.
5. On 15 December 1947.
6. Sardar here refers to Gandhiji's visit to Banaras Hindu University on 4 February 1916 at its opening ceremony when Gandhiji had delivered a speech that had irked Dr. Annie Besant and many among the Princely Order for his pungent remarks on India's crushing poverty amidst that pomp and glory.
7. Penance.
8. In the Interim Government.
9. Jawaharlal Nehru.
10. Indian Independence Legislation, 1947.
11. Banaras merged into U. P. on 15.10.49
12. A man of great piety and erudite scholarship.

WHO'S WHO

Abbas, Taiyabji: Retired Judge of Baroda State and well-known freedom fighter; was a close associate of Mahatma Gandhi and Vallabhbhai Patel; became President of the Kaira D.C.C. and elected to the A.I.C.C. [1923].

Abdul Ghaffar Khan: Known as *Badshah Khan* and the *Frontier Gandhi*; was organizer of the *Khudai Khidmatgar* in the N.W.F.P. and the Red Shirt Movement [1930]; appointed member C.W.C. [1936-1947].

Ambedkar, B. R.: Eminent lawyer and intellectual who was a member of Viceroy's Council in early years of forties, and the Chairman of Drafting Committee of the Indian Constitution; became the Law Minister of free India [1947].

Amtus Salaam: A well-known freedom fighter and one of Mahatma Gandhi's associates.

Ayyangar, N. Gopalaswami: A senior I. C. S. who worked as the Prime Minister of the State of Jammu and Kashmir [till 1947]; was a minister in the Union Government headed by Jawaharlal Nehru [1947-1953].

Azad, Abul Kalam: Nationalist and a prominent Congress leader and freedom fighter; edited ***Vakil*** of Amritsar, Al-Hilal and Al-Balagh; became President of Indian National Congress in its Delhi Session [1923] and at Ramgarh [1940]; appointed minister for Education in free India's first government [1947].

Bhave, Vinoba: Eminent Gandhian, Bhoodan-leader and intellectual who took part at the Nagpur Flag *Satyagraha* [1923]; was declared as the first *Satyagrahi* in 1940 by Mahatma Gandhi on the eve of Individual Civil Disobedience.

Bose, Subhas Chandra: Affectionately called as '*Netaji*', a patriot and front ranking Congress leader from Bengal; elected President of the Indian National Congress twice at Haripura [1938] and Tripuri [1939]; founded the Forward Block, the Indian National Army and the Indian National Government during the World War Second; imprisoned several times during national liberation movement.

Desai, Mahadev Harilal: Well-known scholar and Private Secretary to Mahatma Gandhi; died at the Ahmednagar Fort [1943].

Desai, Morarji Ranchhorji: Prominent Congress leader and freedom fighter from Gujarat; was a minister in the State of Bombay [1937 and 1946]; became Chief Minister of the State [1952] and later joined the Union Cabinet, headed by Nehru and Indira Gandhi; served as the Prime Minister of India [1977-79].

Diwakar, R. R.: Prominent Congressman and freedom fighter from Karnataka; took over from Sardar Patel as minister of state for Information and Broadcasting [1948]; appointed Governor of Bihar [1952].

Gadgil, N. V.: Front ranking freedom fighter and the Congress leader from Maharashtra; became a minister in the first Cabinet of independent India [1947]; appointed Governor of undivided Punjab [1958].

Gandhi, M. K.: Supreme leader of the Indian National Movement for freedom and the I. N. C. [1920-1947]; elected President of the Congress [1924]; was Editor of Young India, Navajivan, Harijan Sewak and Harijan [1919-1948].

Gajendragadkar, P.V.: Chief Justice of India early in the sixties.

Haksar, P. N.: A noted diplomat, who, during Indira Gandhi's regime served as the Vice-Chairman of the Planning Commission of India also.

Jinnah, Muhammad Ali: A prominent leader of the Muslim League and the first Governor General of Pakistan [1947]; was elected to the Indian Legislative Assembly in 1930 and 1934.

Khare, Narayan Bhaskar: Well-known Congressman from the Central Provinces who lead the Congress Ministry in the State [1937-1938].

Mavalankar, G.V.: Leading lawyer of Ahmedabad and a Congressman from Gujarat; was a Secretary of the *Gujarat Sabha* [1918], the G. P. C. C. [1921-1922]; became Speaker of the Bombay Legislative Assembly and later the President of Central Legislative Assembly [1946]; elected Speaker of the first Lok Sabha [1952].

Mashruwala Kishorlal: A well known Gandhian Scholar and thinker.

Mountbatten, L.: Viceroy and Governor-General of India [March-August 1947]; worked as the Governor-General of the Indian Dominion from August 1947 to June 1948.

Munshi, K.M.: Renowned advocate of Bombay and Congress leader; was a member of the Bombay Legislative Council; became Agent-General of India in the State of Hyderabad [1948]; joined Union Cabinet and later appointed the Governor of U. P.

Nehru, Jawaharlal: Leading freedom fighter; elected the President of the Indian National Congress [1929, 1936, 1937 and 1946]; founded All India *Kisan Sabha, Bharat Krishak Samaj*; lead the country as the Prime Minister [1946-1964].

Pant, Govind Ballabh: Well-known freedom fighter and Congressman from United Provinces; elected to the Central Legislative Assembly [1934]; became Premier of the State of U. P. [1937 and 1946], and the Chief Minister [1947], and later minister for Home Affairs in the Government of India.

Patel, Manibehn Vallabhbhai: Daughter of Sardar Vallabhbhai Patel; was a renowned freedom fighter and social worker; elected several times to the both Houses of Parliament between 1952 and 1977.

Patel, Vithalbhai J.: Well-known barrister of Bombay and elder brother of Sardar Patel; was a top ranking freedom fighter and the Congress leader; elected Speaker of the Central Legislative Assembly in 1925.

Prasad, Rajendra: A leading Congress leader, freedom fighter and constructive worker from Bihar, elected President of the Indian National Congress [1935]; appointed Food and Agriculture Minister in the Interim Government [1946]; elected Chairman of the Constituent Assembly [1947]; became the President of the Indian Republic [1950, 1952 and 1957].

Rajagopalachari, C.: Front-ranking Congressman from Madras and a Gandhian thinker; became the Premier of the State [1937]; appointed Governor of West Bengal [1947], the Governor-General of India [1948] and Minister for Home Affairs [1950].

Shaikh Abdullah: A prominent leader of Kashmir Valley and the All Jammu and Kashmir Muslim Conference; was imprisoned by the Ruler of the State for the 'Quit Kashmir Movement' [1946]; lead the interim government of the State [1947]; became the Premier [1948]; removed from the office by Karan Singh-the *Sadar-i-Riyasat* of the State and detained [1953]; became Chief Minister of the state again [1975].

Shiva Rao, B.: A leading Congressman from Andhra; was a member of the Indian Constituent Assembly.

Singh, Tara: One of the top Akali Party leaders from Punjab; launched agitation for a separate State for the Sikh community.

Sitaramayya B. Pattabhi: Front ranking Congress leader from Andhra; became the President of the A.I.C.C. in 1948.

Tilak, Bal Gangadhar: Great Congress leader from Maharashtra; was a leading figure of *Swadeshi* Movement [1905]; edited ***Maratha*** and ***Kesari***; imprisoned several times during national liberation movement.

Yagnik, Indulal: One of the renowned political and constructive workers of Gujarat; was a Secretary of the G.P.C.C. [1921-1922]; took part in the freedom movement; elected to the Lok Sabha.

Zakir Hussain: A Noted educationist who served as the Vice-President of India [1962-1967] and later as the President of the Indian Republic [1967-1969].

Glossary of Indian Terms

Abhinandan : Ceremonial greetings; praise Commemoration; Applause

Ahimsa : Non-violence

Anna : Former coin of India; 1/16 of a rupee

Aryan : Honourable; Noble; One who belongs to Aryan race; Excellent

Ashram : Hermitage; Abode; One of the four stages in the Vedic-Hindu's life

Aatmiyata : Feeling of kinship of intimacy; Nearness; Close relationship or friendship

Bagh : A garden

Babu : A clerk

Brahmcharya : Observance of chastity or continuence in quest of Truth, that is, God

Brahmin : A member of highest or priestly class among Hindus

Buniyadi : Basic

Charkha : Spinning-wheel

Darbar : A royal court; Hall of audience; Holding of a court; Royal audience; A ruler

Dharma : Religious injunction; Religion; Duty

Gaddi : A seat

Ghee : Clarified butter

Gita, the : The Celestial Song, highly philosophical poem laying emphasis on the selfless view of life and action

Granth : A volume; A literary work; A book; Treatise

Goshala : A cow-shed; A cow tending centre

Halpati : A cultivator

Harijan : Literally child of God; A name coined by Mahatma Gandhi to describe the so-called Untouchables

Hartal : Suspension of work as a mark of protest or mourning; Strike

Katha : A story

Khadi : Hand spun hand- woven cloth

Kisan : A peasant; Farmer

Kranti : Revolution; Progress; Development; Course of the sun on the ecliptic

Krishak : A peasant; Farmer

Kshatriya : A warrior; A member of the Second of the four Hindu [Vedic] Varnas

Lok : The world; the Universe; People; Folk; Public; Society

Maharaja : The ruler of a former India State of a large territory such as Jammu and Kashmir

Mahasabha : A great council; Senate; General Assembly or Council

Mahatma : High souled; Of noble nature; A noble or venerable man; A ṭitle bestowed on Mahatma Gandhi- the father of the Indian nation

Majlis : An assembly; A Muslim body; Organization; Legislature; Parliament

Mandal : A circle; A division comprising of some districts; Globe; Sphere; Association; Gathering

Maulana : A title of respect applied to learned Muslim

Mazdoor : A labourer; A workman

Nishkamakarmayoga : Pertaining to the philosophy of selfless service as propounded in Srimad Bhagvad-Gita

Patel : Village headman

Patra : Magazine; Journal

Patidar : A popular community of agriculturists of Centra Gujarat

Praja-Parishad : People's assembly or organization

Rabi : The spring crop or harvest

Rajpramukh : The constitutional head of the interim unions of States just after independence of India

Rajya : A State; Province; Rule; Kingdom; Government; Sway

Rani : Queen

Sabha : Assembly; Meeting; Gathering; A society; An association; A deliberative body; Council; A house

Samaj : A society; Association; Community

Sammelan : A conference

Sangh : An association; Group; Community; Body; Union; Party; Federation; Sect; A community of Buddhist or Jain monks; An Organization; Buddhist monastery or convent

Sardar : A leader; Captain; A title bestowed on Vallabhbhai Patel after the triumph of the Bardoli *Kisan Satyagraha* in 1928

Sarvodaya : Universal good

Satyagraha : Literally holding on to Truth; Truth-force or soul-force; Mahatma Gandhi's weapon of Truth and Love for mass action

Sewak : A servant

Suba : A province; State

Subedar : Governor of a province; A captain

Swadeshi : Belonging to one's own country; Specific; Manufactured in one's own country; Not imported; Country made; In economics the doctrine of preferential use of the products of one's own country

Swaraj or Swarajya : Self-rule; Independence; Mahatma Gandhi's conception of social, political and economic freedom in true sense of the term

Talati : A village revenue officer concerned with the collection of land revenue

Taluka : Also known as the Tehsil; An administrative unit of varying sizes, usually extending over a few square miles in area and comprising of a number of villages and one or two towns

Varnas : Occupational division of Vedic Hindu society in four parts

Vasudhaiva Kutumbakam : Vedic concept to universal brotherhood [whole world is but one family]

Vidya : Knowledge; Learning; A field of knowledge; Skill; Art; Study; Spell

Vidyapeeth : A university; A deemed university or an institution or a college equivalent to a university

Vikas : Development; Progress

Vir : A brave; Heroic; Mighty; A worrier; A hero; A righteous man

Yoga : A theory or practice of abstract meditation undertaken to bring the soul towards or into union with the Supreme spirit; Bodily exercise or disciplines; A connotation; Union; Combination; Conjuncture; Agreement; Similarity; Application

Zamindar : A landlord

Index

H

I

L

M

N